MURDER & MAYHEM IN TUCSON

MURDER & MAYHEM IN TUCSON

PATRICK WHITEHURST

FOREWORD BY CRIME FICTION AUTHOR TOM PITTS

THE History PRESS

Published by The History Press
Charleston, SC
www.historypress.com

Cover image: Panorama of Tucson and vicinity, Arizona. *West Coast Art Company, Copyright Claimant. Panorama of Tucson & Vicinity, Arizona. United States, Tucson, Arizona, ca. 1909. Photograph. https://www.loc.gov/item/2007661397.*

First published 2021

Manufactured in the United States

ISBN 9781467146289

Library of Congress Control Number: 2021941088

For my son, Ben. You're the best of the best.

CONTENTS

Contents

FOREWORD

I'm often asked what lured me to crime fiction. Interviewers want to know what dark path led me to the visceral chaos that populates my books. It's no secret—it took a long, steady diet of true crime to skew my worldview. More so than the memoir or historical fiction, nonfiction—specifically crime fiction—allows us a peek into the dark psyche that is the human condition. If Mother Nature can be a cruel and unpredictable force, then human nature can be insidious, sinful, selfish and, as history proves, consistent.

I'd read Patrick's ghostly guide to Monterey, California, so when he told me that he was assembling a history of murder and mayhem in Tucson, I knew that two of my interests would be served together: the spectral float through history with the bite of true crime. What Patrick didn't realize was that, along with my prurient interests in any kind of felonious follies, I also have a personal tie-in with the criminal Tucson.

As a fiction writer, I'm envious of nonfiction, with its uncorkable muse and predetermined outlines. I'm not, however, envious of the effort it takes. It was a failed attempt at journalism that steered me toward fiction in the first place. I discovered that factual reportage was not my strong suit, mostly because I couldn't do the heavy lifting. In the early '90s, I buried myself in books about organized crime. I was so overinformed when it came to America's Mafia that I thought I could teach a course. Friends insisted I should try to write my own tome about the history of La Cosa Nostra in San Francisco. Problem was, the only thing I knew about writing a book was how to read one. I had no idea where a real writer would start, so—with the help of the Tucson phone book (remember those?)—I chased down the famous FBI agent William Roemer, the storied agent who'd gained fame battling Sam Giancana. Roemer had also retired to Tucson, alongside his neighbor and nemesis Joe "Bananas" Bonanno, whose own Tucson saga is detailed in this book. The voice I'd heard interviewed in countless gangster documentaries answered on the second ring. Ultimately, my story got shut down by the San Francisco Federal Bureau of Investigation, but that's another story.

The real connection I have with Tucson's underworld is considerably less glamorous and not nearly as far up the criminal ladder. Renowned for rehabs and retirees, Tucson is often thought of as an anemic Southwest desert town by those who've never visited. I know better. I've personally enjoyed the fortifying experience of trolling the Southside looking for hookers beat down enough by life that they'd know where to find cheap heroin. So—via several wild goose chases through the criminal underbelly of Tucson—I was able to see the Arizona I missed as a boy while tooling around Scottsdale in the back of my mother's station wagon. When it comes to the rough-and-tumble, Tucson is at the front of the pack with the big burgs.

For the longest time, it seemed like most of the murder and mayhem were reserved for the coasts. Places like Arizona were placeholders for tales of the Wild West. But it's not just New York or Los Angeles—it's the cities between, places like Tucson, where the real fabric of true crime is sewn. Gentrified urban centers have priced out all but those who can afford them, and that means the criminals too. What used to be considered the safe suburbs is now the canvas for the new legends. The smaller cities and their outer environs are where the great middle now sits. It's where the hunger, the struggle of Americans, still exists.

Knowing your history is more than when bills were passed or wars were won; it's tasting those ingredients that went into the wonderful tempest that is America. Nonfiction is the real data from the human experiment. It's those stories that people really want, the lessons they teach. The next time you're at the airport, note the percentage of nonfiction to fiction on the bestsellers shelf. Fiction is only a hypothesis. With nonfiction, there are no lingering doubts about plausibility. The boundaries of behavior are marked by how far people have been willing to push them—not hypothetically, not theoretically, but in reality, that painful plane where we all struggle, live and learn from our past.

Foreword

If truth is stranger than fiction, then true crime is definitely more frightening, more threatening than the fictional bad guys dreamed up by writers safely sequestered in comfortable rooms. As much as we enjoy the timeless battle between good and evil being played out on a stage, there is no comparison to the empathetic connection one feels when the players are people, the stakes are real and the stories are true.

—Tom Pitts

PREFACE

Edgar Allan Poe likely had no idea of the floodgates he'd bust open when he wrote what is largely considered the first detective story, "The Murders in the Rue Morgue," in 1841. It is at least the most well-known source when it comes to the search for an origin. Truman Capote is thought to be the father of modern true crime books thanks to his book *In Cold Blood*. Today, studies in true crime offer insight and details that may be lacking elsewhere. They're a way for us to connect with the past and learn from it. In writing *Murder & Mayhem in Tucson*, I learned a great deal about the city of Tucson, both good and bad, and am proud to call this community home.

Thanks to Paul Van de Carr, artist extraordinaire, for his photo assistance with this project. Thanks also to History Press acquisitions editor Laurie Krill and all the good folks under the Arcadia Publishing banner. Fellow *Murder & Mayhem* author Teresa Nordheim has my thanks for letting me pick her brain as I embarked on this adventure. And, as always, thanks to my family, for giving me the space to delve into these often uncomfortable events.

Thank you to Tom Pitts, author of *Cold Water* and other fantastic crime fiction novels, for penning the foreword to this book. He's truly one of the best breathing crime writers out there today.

PROLOGUE

EARLY TUCSON

WELCOME TO THE OLD PUEBLO

Tucson is a Spanish version of the O'odham word *Cuk Ṣon*, roughly meaning "at the base of the black hill." About twelve thousand years ago, the area around Tucson was home to Paleoindians, who farmed the land, hunted in the scrub and gathered wild nuts and plants to eat. The Hohokam cultural group also called the area home between AD 600 and AD 1450.

Tucson is a community like no other. With lush deserts tucked neatly between the Santa Catalina and Santa Rita Mountains, it's the second-largest city in the state of Arizona, just below the city of Phoenix, located more than one hundred miles to the north. The Mexico border is situated about sixty miles to the south. There are more than 500,000 residents in the sprawling city, with some estimates reporting more than 1 million when you add outlying areas like Oro Valley and Marana to the mix. For a time, it held the title of being the state's largest community. Like all cities, Tucson has had its share of death and chaos since its beginnings in the eighteenth century.

Once called Presidio San Agustín del Tucsón, Tucson began as a Spanish military complex and remained so until Mexico gained independence from Spain in 1821. The original fort was founded by Irishman Hugh O'Conor, who in 1775 selected the site for Spain. The British use the word *fort* to replace the word *castle* to describe fortified structures surrounded by walls and guarded by armed troops. The exact location of the settlement is today found near the current site of the Pima County Courthouse. After 1821, Tucson became part of the Mexican state of Sonora for a little more than thirty years. In 1854, the United States got its hands on Tucson as part of the Gadsden Purchase.

In 1779, while still in its Spanish fort days, the community saw its first episode of violence when soldiers engaged in combat with the Apaches of the region in what's known as the First Battle of Tucson. It was followed a few short years later by the larger Second Battle of Tucson. More battles would follow over the course of Tucson's history.

Tucson mayor Sidney Randolph DeLong was the first person to be elected to the position in 1871. He was elected for a one-year term. *Findagrave.com.*

Often referred to as the "Old Pueblo," Tucson is today a thriving, diverse community and serves as the base for Pima County in which it sits. It's also home to the University of Arizona, founded in 1885 as the first of its kind in the Arizona Territory. As with any growing community, criminal activity would become a part of life in old Tucson. While the death penalty in Arizona has been suspended twice, there have been one hundred state-sanctioned executions here. Capital punishment was first suspended at the end of 1916 and then reinstated in 1918. It was again suspended in 1962 but brought back in 1992. Jose Lopez made history in Arizona as the first man to be officially executed in the state. He died the morning of January 5, 1910. Eva Dugan, meanwhile, was the first woman to be executed in Arizona. She was hanged in the early morning hours of February 21, 1930. Those who monitor the Thin Blue Line are not immune to death in the line of duty. Between 1892 and 2008, eight officers have lost their lives in the line of duty, beginning with William Elliott, who was stabbed to death on July 3, 1892, leaving behind a wife and two children.

The horrors of war brought many to Tucson in the early 1900s, particularly those seeking sunshine and clean air in which to heal. For two decades, Tucson was deemed something of a health resort for soldiers poisoned by mustard gas in World War I. It was also known as a haven for those suffering from general ill health and tuberculosis in particular. Tucson's attraction became stronger with the invention of the swamp cooler, allowing cooler air to circulate indoors no matter the outside temperatures. Soldiers from World War II also made their way to the Southwest, creating a population boom in the Tucson community.

Tragedies are never victimless. Families suffered as a result of the horrific incidents detailed within the pages of this book, and in writing it, I tried

Downtown Tucson as it appears today. The city was founded as a Spanish fort in 1775 but became a part of the United States via the Gadsden Purchase in 1854. *Author's collection.*

to honor their memories as much as possible. These stories of murder and mayhem are only some of the tales found in and around the community of Tucson, but I hope they serve as a proper sampling of the darker side of this city's historical makeup—a characteristic known to all cities across this vast country. Ralph Waldo Emerson once said, "When it is dark enough, you can see the stars." I like to think he means that we can all rise up, through pain and despair, to become better.

May we all become stars in our own right.

THE BATTLES OF TUCSON

BLOODSHED AMONG THE SAGUARO

Little is known about the first battle of Tucson, Arizona, only that a group of fifteen brave men fought tooth and nail against an army of more than three hundred warriors. According to historians, the deadly confrontation began on December 6, 1779, when an army of Apache warriors descended on the Tucson Fort, which was commanded by Spanish captain Pedro Allande y Saabedra. The fort was located in the Sonoran Desert and is now located within the city limits of Tucson. There was nothing save cactus and the denizens of the desert at that time, however, save what the Spanish soldiers built with their own hands. When it came to the attack, they had only one another to rely on. Their Spanish lancers successfully defended the fort.

Lancers, named for their use of a long combat weapon, have been a military fixture throughout history. Beginning back in the 700s, Assyrians were believed to be the first to use the weapons in combat. Lances were used by Greeks, Romans, Chinese and other dominant civilizations. Lancers were also deployed during the Middle Ages and Renaissance, and less deadly versions can still be seen at local Renaissance festivals throughout the world.

The First Battle of Tucson is considered to be a chapter in the bloody, long-running Apache-Mexico Wars, fought between the early 1600s and finally coming to an end around 1915. The wars began when the Spanish colonized the land where New Mexico is located today. What first began as an amicable relationship between the two cultures crumbled to dust when slavers began to raid Native American camps. Apaches raided a number of Spanish settlements as well. By the 1770s, the conflict had grown in size and scope. The Spanish fortified their northern borders with the creation of presidios, a series of which could be found in Sonora, Chihuahua, Texas, New Mexico and in what would become known as the Arizona Territory. A presidio would be built in Tucson, the Presidio San Augustin del Tucson, that became the most important installation in the state. Historians believe that the conflict reached its peak between 1771 and 1776, when in Coahuila and Chihuahua the Spanish claimed that more than 1,600 of their people had been killed in Apache battles. As casualties mounted on both sides, Mexico City viceroy Bernardo de Galvez instructed in 1786 that efforts be made at both war and peace where possible.

Seven years earlier, however, deadly raids were the norm in the Southwest. The battles, such as that fought in Tucson that December in 1776, were so bloodthirsty that it's said Allande decapitated the head from a dead Apache chieftain and carried it on the tip of a lance as a trophy. He waved the gruesome sight at the remaining warriors, who quickly fled the battle after witnessing the head of their slain leader. A death count for that first battle was never made clear.

THE SECOND BATTLE OF TUCSON

A small garrison of Spanish soldiers found themselves facing the same threat a handful of years later when hundreds of Apache warriors once again attacked the presidio. For years, smaller skirmishes had been fought in the Tucson area, as Apache warriors raided convoys and wagon trains that were less guarded.

The Second Battle of Tucson, however, presented a graver threat than the first, as the Apaches marshaled their forces into a massive army of about six hundred fighters. Allande once again found himself facing a much larger enemy, although he had worked after the first attack to fortify the area around the presidio to defend against subsequent attacks. When the second battle occurred, on May 1, 1782, also known as the May Day Attack, the fort featured significant upgrades to help repel invaders.

Construction on Fort Tucson occurred a year before the First Battle of Tucson and continued until 1783. Upon completion, the compound featured a fort of adobe bricks, a muddy block made of organic materials and mesquite wood. It had a garrison of soldiers made up of anywhere from

A sketch of the gates at the Tucson Presidio as they might have appeared to visitors and residents in the late 1700s. *Center for Desert Archaeology.*

forty to seventy troops, some of whom armed a powerful cannon. Adobe structures known as jacals dotted the land around Fort Tucson. They were surrounded by wooden stakes that formed a fence around the neighborhood. Workers constructed a ditch around portions of the land that they filled with water. Ramparts were also erected, as were bulwarks, guard towers and a church. Walls around Fort Tucson ranged from ten to thirty feet in height.

These fortifications made attacks more difficult for smaller bands of aggressors, leading to the Apaches gathering in larger numbers for concentrated raids. The surprise May Day Attack formed a resounding, strong response to Spanish incursions in Apache territory, according to historical accounts. The battle began at roughly 10:00 a.m. when two Apache groups raided the nearby Pima Pueblo, known as Indian Town, and the fort itself simultaneously. Fighting occurred at three main points: the bridge that connected the pueblo to the fort, the western gate to the fort and the western gate to one of the Spanish lieutenant's home. It's said that the Spanish contingent consisted of seventy-two soldiers: forty-two soldiers with lances, twenty mounted soldiers and ten native officers.

The Spanish garrison, while smaller than the invading Apache army, managed to hold the bridge due to superior firepower in close-quarters combat. Allande, with four men, repelled Apaches who rushed the open western gate with cannon and musket fire. The May Day Attack, in all, lasted two hours and left eight Apache men dead and an untold number wounded. One Spanish soldier and a civilian woman were also killed in the attack. The Apaches withdrew before more deaths occurred. Some accounts, which varied among Jesuit priests stationed there for soldiers in the field, indicated that as many as thirty Apaches were killed in the fighting and that many of the dead and wounded were carried off by their comrades. Allande himself is said to have killed two raiders during the fighting. Most accounts of the battles were from the Spanish citizens and those living among them.

THE THIRD BATTLE OF TUCSON

Despite retreating from the May Day Attack, the Apaches would again face down the Spanish soldiers from Fort Tucson. This time, the Apaches raided a cattle herd and clashed with troops under Allande's command on Christmas Day 1782. The conflict has since become known as the Third Battle of Tucson.

Six Apache warriors were believed killed during the fighting that ensued, with an unknown number of Spanish casualties. The cattle, according to Spanish records, were ultimately recovered. In a brutal show of force, Allande also severed the heads of the dead Apaches and placed them on the walls of the fort in an effort to deter further raids.

THE FOURTH BATTLE OF TUCSON

Two years after the cattle raid, Apache and Navajo warriors combined into a raiding party that numbered about five hundred. With a large force at their command, the warriors raided the fort to steal livestock, which were under the protection of the Spanish soldiers stationed there. The attack began at sunrise on March 21, 1784, with stealing the fort's horses being the Apaches' only goal. Under the leadership of Ensign Don Juan Carrillo, the Spanish managed to slow the Apache/Navajo force for some time but were unable to stop the attackers from stampeding the horses and making off with them. By the time the fighting ended, five Spanish soldiers lay dead and thirteen horses had been taken. Three of the invading force were killed, in addition to sustaining other casualties, although an exact count was never determined.

Wasting no time, the Spanish mounted a retrieval party consisting of forty-nine men. They immediately set out to follow the trail left by the raiding party. According to most accounts, it took only forty-five minutes to catch up to the warriors. The subsequent clash occurred at the base of the Santa Catalina Mountains, located north of Tucson, and took the lives of fourteen members of the Apache/Navajo band, according to accounts.

THE STORY OF THE SAN XAVIER MISSION

HISTORIC SITE IS HOME TO RELICS AND TRAGEDY

Father Eusebio Kino founded San Xavier as a Catholic Mission in 1692, but it would be some years later before the current structure would appear there. The religious structure was originally built to repel Apache attacks and provide more safety to those who lived there. By the time the current buildings appeared, the Mission had been a fixture in the area for almost a century. Besides being a site of historical significance in the Southwest, the site retains its primary mission of service to its parishioners.

The Mission San Xavier del Bac, also known as the "White Dove of the Desert," began after Father Juan Bautista Velderrain borrowed money from a Sonoran rancher to create a grand Spanish Colonial structure for the Tucson area. The income allowed him to hire an architect and work crews to begin construction on the Mission as it appears now. Church officials adorned the interior with statuary and murals from the eighteenth century, much of which can still be viewed inside.

With Mexico's independence in 1821, the Mission became a part of that country for more than thirty years. With the Gadsden Purchase of 1854, however, it became a part of the United States, and the church was folded into the Diocese of Santa Fe. It became a diocese itself in 1866, and since 1872, the Franciscan Sisters of Christian Charity have taught at the Mission. Franciscans, the last of which left in 1837, stepped back into the fold in 1913. Restoration of the Mission has been underway for a number of years and continues to this day. The site has also become a nonprofit organization.

The Mission San Xavier del Bac is located about ten miles south of downtown Tucson. It was founded in 1692 by Padre Eusebio Kino. *Author's collection.*

Today, more than twenty thousand visitors make their way to the Mission each year. The Mission itself is a National Historic Landmark and is one of the area's oldest, and still standing, structures in the state.

The coat of arms of the Franciscan order hangs above one of the entries to the Mission. The façade features a shell just above the entry, and just above that is found the coat of arms. On it a mouse and a cat can be seen on two scrolls. The façade was sculpted by Augustino Marquez. According to legend, should the cat ever reach the mouse, the world will come to an end.

To date, the cat has yet to reach that mouse, although tragedy has managed to find its way to the Mission over the area's long history. Natural disasters have occurred there on numerous occasions, including an earthquake in 1887. The quake toppled a wall at the mortuary and damaged the church itself, leading to extensive repair work at the time under the supervision of Bishop Henry Granjon. In 1939, further restoration work began after lightning struck the lantern on the west tower. Other weather disasters would prove even deadlier.

On August 27, 1964, a tornado ripped through the area nine miles south of downtown Tucson. Newspaper accounts of the incident called it

Artist Augustino Marquez made the façade found on the entry to the mission. On it can be found a mouse and a cat atop two scrolls. According to legend, should the cat ever catch the mouse, the world will end. *Author's collection.*

a small but deadly tornado. Two lives were lost as the twister tore through the meager structures located around the Mission. Lucy Norris and her infant son, Marcian Norris, were both killed. Members of her family were also injured when the tornado crashed into their adobe home, located a scant two hundred yards from the Mission. The local weather bureau at the time claimed that it was the first tornado in Arizona's history to claim human lives.

Ten years later, a second tornado would appear, this time north of the Mission. It would claim another life. In late June 1974, a tornado cut a swath of destruction through the Jamar Trailer Court near South Cardinal Road, killing one person, seventy-eight-year-old Carl Fehr. Fehr was found crushed to death under a pile of debris left by the funnel. The tornado flipped vehicles and flattened more than ten mobile homes. First responders to the scene included the Tucson Fire Department, the Pima County Sheriff's Department, the Drexel Heights Volunteer Fire Department, Pima County Search and Rescue and the American Red Cross. The 1974 tornado was deemed an F1 on the Fujita scale. The rating system was developed in 1971 by Ted Fujita of the University of Chicago and was later replaced by the Enhanced Fujita Scale (EF) in 2007. The 1974 tornado was the last tornado in the Tucson area to take a human life. Besides one fatality, about forty residents were injured as a result. In all, it left seventy-five people homeless. Weather reports indicated at the time that there were two cells, although only one caused major devastation in its wake. Police and other responders reported funnel clouds at a number of locations during the storm. It wouldn't be the last weather event to threaten the Tucson community.

THE CAMP GRANT MASSACRE

TUCSON'S FEAR OF THE APACHES

One of the area's bloodiest massacres occurred about sixty miles north of Tucson at a spot known as Camp Grant. The massacre occurred during a period when Apache warriors fought against many enemies, including Mexicans and American settlers. This included the Battles of Tucson detailed earlier. The Camp Grant Massacre was one of the worst of its kind and remains a stain on southern Arizona's history.

Camp Grant housed a number of Apaches hailing from the Aravaipa and Pinal tribes. These families had surrendered to the camp in trade for supplies. It's said that as many as five hundred Apaches came in peace to the camp. There they worked the hay for the soldiers' horses and worked the fields, harvesting crops to pay for the supplies. Many, including the commanding officer of the camp, Lieutenant Royal Emerson Whitman, said that the Native Americans there had nothing to do with recent deadly raids in that part of the Arizona Territory. According to Whitman, those entering and leaving the camp were counted, leaving little doubt as to their whereabouts. Had they been involved in attacks, Whitman believed that he would have known. But in the minds of some Tucsonans, the truth mattered little. What mattered more to them was that the people living in the camp were Apache, and they feared that they could discard their peaceful ways and attack at any time.

A group calling themselves the Tucson Committee of Public Safety, organized by a coalition of six white Tucsonans led by William Oury, and a group of forty-two Mexicans, led by Jesús María Elías, enlisted the

John Karl Hillers, a photographer with the U.S. Army, took this 1870 photograph of Camp Grant near Tucson. A massacre would occur there one year later. *Library of Congress.*

aid of ninety-two members of the Tohono O'odham tribe to accompany them to the camp on April 28, 1871. Their intent? Eliminate the perceived Apache threat. Although the group was larger at the outset, a number of individuals, it's said, thought better of the horrific attack and stayed home rather than participate.

The committee made use of the fact that the Apaches had recently moved their small dwellings and had not completely settled into their new surroundings. They'd just relocated to an area upstream from the main camp. Whitman himself approved the move. To prepare, the attackers blocked the military road leading to the camp. The attacking force accessed the Apache settlement by way of a trail over Redington Pass.

Once there, the group surrounded the largely defenseless encampment and, before sunrise, carried out their murderous assault. Women and children were slaughtered, many while they were waking, when the brutal attack tore through the camp. Many of Grant's male inhabitants were hunting for a forthcoming party (which Whitman had allegedly encouraged) and therefore were not there to defend their families and friends. Only eight of those killed were men, the rest women and children. Some were shot as they fled the settlement to raise the alarm at the main camp. Unfortunately, because they had moved, their cries were not immediately heard by the soldiers stationed at the camp. It's estimated that between 80 and 140 were murdered that morning—an exact number is not known. The members of the Tucson Committee of Public Safety used guns, knives and clubs in the attack, according to historical records, and made off with at least thirty of the camp's children. Many of the adolescents were taken into the households of their captors to work as servants, while others were sold off as slave labor in

Sonora. It's said that very few Apaches survived the massacre that morning. Many of those who did went into hiding in the nearby mountains.

Whitman, who eventually learned of the attack, arrived too late to help anyone. Back in Tucson, meanwhile, news of the massacre was a cause for celebration for those who agreed with the murderous committee. Others quickly sought to indict those responsible for the deed. President Ulysses S. Grant was said to have called the attack "purely murder." And while a trial eventually occurred, with about one hundred defendants, a Tucson jury quickly dealt a verdict of not guilty and the men were freed. Over time, sentiments changed, however, even among some of the men who took part in the attack, with some saying that they regretted their actions that morning. One such man, Sidney DeLong, who would later be elected Tucson mayor, said that his biggest regret in life was taking part in the massacre. A delegation of Tucsonans in 1996 visited the San Carlos Reservation to officially apologize to the Apache people for the deeds of early residents. The site of the massacre is listed in the National Register of Historic Places.

GERONIMO'S RAIDS

TUCSON'S CONNECTION TO THE INFAMOUS APACHE LEADER

Geronimo's story is a famous one among historians, Native Americans and fans of southwestern lore.

Named Goyathlay (or Goyahkla), his Apache name means "One Who Yawns," although the man's life was anything but boring. Born in June 1829 in No-Doyohn Canyon, Mexico, he was raised as a Bedonkohe, part of the Chiricahua Apache tribe. Enemies surrounded their tribal land. These ranged from Navajo to Comanches, Mexicans and more. His land would later become part of the United States in New Mexico and Arizona.

The Apaches would often raid their neighboring communities, leading to bad blood between the varied groups. Legends grew around the young Goyathlay as he matured among the Apache people, including one story that says he ate the heart of his kill after his first hunt. This, according to legend, was done to ensure a lifetime of success. By his seventeenth birthday, the young Geronimo had already engaged in four raids on neighboring lands. At this time, Apache raids led to bounties being offered for the scalps of any member of the tribe, including children.

While still young, Geronimo fell in love with a woman named Alope, and the two married. They had three children together as well, although their new life would be short-lived, as fate had other plans for the youthful warrior. The children and Alope were killed by Mexican soldiers while many of the Apache men were on a trading trip and not present to defend the camp, Geronimo among them. Their deaths are said to have had a profound effect on the young man. Per tradition, he burned the family's belongings

An 1887 photograph of Apache chieftain Geronimo as he kneels with a rifle in his hands. Geronimo was raised as a Bedonkohe, part of the Chiricahua Apache tribe. *Bettmann Archives/Getty Images.*

and retreated into the wilderness to mourn their passing. There, it is said, he heard a voice urging him to attack his enemies, one that indicated, "No gun will ever kill you."

Following his retreat, Geronimo emerged a new man. He gathered an army of two hundred men and immediately set out to find the Mexican soldiers who raided his camp. His rampage of revenge against the Mexican government would continue for ten years, and it's said that he carried a deep hatred for Mexico's people until his death due to the murder of his wife and children. These intense raids were a part of the long-running conflict between the Apaches and Mexico, commonly known as either the Mexican Apache Wars or the Apache-Mexico Wars, which included the Battles of Tucson discussed earlier.

How the young man became known as Geronimo is a hotly disputed topic among historians. It's commonly believed that he earned the moniker after raids against his Mexican neighbors. But where did the name originate? Some believe that Mexican soldiers invoked the name of the Catholic saint Jerome when facing the Apaches in battle, while others believe it was a nickname given to him by Mexican soldiers. Still others think the name emerged from a simpler mistake, that of mispronouncing his birth name.

In any event, his attacks turned against the American government by the 1850s, following the government's appropriation of land from Mexico. Some of that land belonged to the Apache people. Despite a short-lived peace led by Geronimo's father-in-law, Cochise, that established a reservation the Apaches were said to favor, a nonviolent future wasn't in the cards. When Cochise passed away a few years later, the Chiricahua reservation was moved to less desirable land to allow settlers to move in. This didn't sit well with Geronimo, and no longer needing to obey his father-in-law's wishes, he struck out again. It was this period where his story grew into legend, as newspapers reported extensively on his raids and his ability to evade capture on many occasions.

Geronimo's sorties continued for years and covered vast areas, including Tucson. The raids kept many Tucson residents in fear for their lives, as the attacks came without warning. Although he was captured multiple times, Geronimo often found a way to lead his charges once again. One such surrender came in April 1877, when he turned himself in to agent John Clum. He was taken to the San Carlos Indian Reservation after his capture but didn't remain there. He soon escaped with a group of Chiricahua Apaches to resume his attacks. His legend only grew.

The famed warrior was finally apprehended, this time for good, in 1886. General Nelson Miles, with an army of five thousand soldiers, captured Geronimo, as well as Chief Naiche and forty Apache warriors. Naiche is considered the last chief of the Chiricahua Apache Indians. It's estimated that the number of soldiers who took part in the apprehension effort made up 25 percent of the U.S. Army at that time. Geronimo and his soldiers surrendered in a canyon near the Mexico border on September 4, 1886. The episode marked the end of the Apache raids after nearly two hundred years of conflict in the area.

To mark the cessation of the violence, Tucson residents celebrated with a boisterous parade. They held a banquet in honor of General Miles and his troops, according to historical records.

Geronimo later died in 1909 in Oklahoma at the Fort Sill hospital, where he was still held as a prisoner of war. His last words, according to the website Biography, were, "I should never have surrendered. I should have fought until I was the last man alive." But Geronimo's story didn't end there.

While it's generally believed that Geronimo was laid to rest at the Oklahoma fort, there are some who believe that his grave was robbed and that some of his bones, including his skull, were stolen and now reside within the confines of a building known as the Tomb in New Haven, Connecticut. It's also alleged by some that none other than Prescott Bush, grandfather and father to two former U.S. presidents, was among those who dug up

Pictured are Geronimo's troops prior to their surrender to General Crook on March 27, 1886. Many are still armed in the photograph. *Library of Congress.*

the bones while undergoing artillery training at the fort. It's said that the bones eventually made their way to Yale University, where they're used to this day in rituals held by the secretive society known as the Order of Skull and Bones. Many have discredited this theory, however, although the stories persist. Most believe that a grave robbing did, in fact, occur, but that the bones unearthed were not those of Geronimo due to a number of factors, including efforts to hide the grave from robbers and confusion as to where he was actually laid to rest.

Over the years, multiple efforts have been launched to move Geronimo's remains to his tribal lands in New Mexico as part of the Native American Graves Protection and Repatriation Act (NAGPRA). While some relatives have made the push to repatriate his remains, other Geronimo descendants disagreed with the plans.

The history of Geronimo can today be found at the Arizona Historical Society's Tucson museum, located on Second Street. There one can view one of the man's rifles, which he surrendered to John Clum on April 21, 1877. The Clum family later donated the rifle to the Arizona Historical Society for preservation.

Geronimo's story, and his legends, became so well known that movies were made about his exploits, including the 1939 film *Geronimo*, featuring actors Andy Devine and Chief Thundercloud. In 1940, the U.S. military began training paratroopers. Soldiers prepared for their first jump at Fort Benning in Georgia. It's believed that the paratroopers viewed the '39 film the night before the historic jump. While many shouted their name as they plunged out of the craft, one soldier opted to shout "Geronimo!" instead, thus leading to the use of the name when leaping from a high perch. Some claimed that Geronimo himself shouted his name when evading capture and that he once leaped from his horse into a river doing just that. Historians, however, discount this particular legend, due to the fact that his real name was Goyathlay, not Geronimo, and as such he would never have shouted the name Geronimo.

Geronimo Plaza was named in his honor. The plaza, found in downtown Tucson near the University of Arizona campus, is home to businesses, restaurants and the nonprofit organization the Marshall Foundation, which owns and operates Main Gate Square, the property in and around the plaza. The foundation is named for Louise Henriette Foucar, who is featured later in this book.

CIVIL WAR COMES TO TUCSON

BATTLE OF PICACHO PASS TAKES A TOLL NORTH OF CITY

The Civil War made quite an impact on southern Arizona, particularly near Picacho Peak. There a short skirmish occurred that left at least three dead and three wounded. Another three soldiers were captured as a result of the battle, which took place about forty miles north of Tucson and sixty miles south of Phoenix. When it comes to the battles fought during the bloody Civil War, the Battle of Picacho Pass counts as the westernmost conflict.

The Civil War, fought on American soil between 1861 and 1865, was the bloodiest conflict in the western world. The Union's victory against the Confederate army ensured that the nation would remain under one flag and also ended the institution of slavery in the country. In all, more than 625,000 lives were lost as a result of the war. A number of battles were fought in that first year of the Civil War, which began in Charleston Harbor's Fort Sumter on April 12, 1861, when the Confederacy launched an attack on Federal soldiers, leading then President Abraham Lincoln to take action. By the spring of 1865, the Confederate army had surrendered, and America returned to a single nation free of the oppression of slavery.

Most battles, of course, were waged on the eastern half of the country, although many soldiers from the Southwest (including Arizona) were drawn into the conflict. It's commonly believed that this lack of troops led the Confederate military to attempt an incursion into the Southwest, where it planned to mine for mineral deposits to fund the army, not to mention gain a foothold on the West Coast.

Above: Pictured in this artist's sketch is the community of Tucson as it appeared around the time of the Civil War in 1864. *Knox Series.*

Right: Confederate army Brigadier General Henry Hopkins Sibley, seen here in this 1865 photograph by Mathew Brady, oversaw the occupation of the Tucson area during the Civil War. *National Park Service.*

Confederate general Henry Sibley sent a force of about one hundred fighting men to Tucson, where they raised the Confederate flag in February 1862. The troops were to serve as a western buffer, a guard against Apache incursions and an early warning system of sorts that would warn Sibley should they come under threat.

By March of that year, the Confederate soldiers had solidified their position and began to learn about Union troop movements in the region. In an attempt to slow the troops, Confederate soldiers burned hay and other supplies along the troop route, although they did encounter some Union resistance that left one soldier wounded. As the Confederate soldiers

Abraham Lincoln, the sixteenth president of the United States, steered the Union through the Civil War. "Honest Abe" issued the Emancipation Proclamation in 1863, which freed slaves in Southern states. *Library of Congress.*

drew back into Tucson, Captain Sherod Hunter posted ten or so troops at Picacho Pass.

Not long after, in early April, Union captain William Calloway made his way to the area with his troops. Determined to take Tucson from the Confederates, he sent two groups to Picacho Pass to monitor the situation. He hoped to take prisoners and learn from them details about the Confederate presence in the area. First Lieutenant James Barrett of the California Cavalry led one of the groups with the help of an advance scout. Although this scout informed him that the troops under Hunter's command were unaware they were being watched, Barrett seemed to have no desire to simply hold the position. Instead, he led a charge into the Confederate camp. The incursion might have ended peacefully, according to historical accounts, only Barrett discharged his weapon at some point during the Confederate surrender.

Believing that there was no intention to take prisoners, the soldiers had no choice but to return fire. For about an hour, war raged between the small groups of fighting men. Barrett was shot in the neck and killed.

Three Confederate soldiers were taken prisoner. In all, Union casualties resulted in one dead and four wounded, with one of them passing the next day. The Union soldiers ultimately withdrew from the battle after running low on ammunition. The Confederates retreated back to Tucson, dashing any hopes of a surprise attack when the Union soldiers eventually made their way to town.

Despite this, the soldiers marched south to take Tucson back from the Confederates. Luckily, the soldiers under the Confederate flag withdrew rather than fight, putting Tucson back in the hands of the North without further bloodshed. The Star and Stripes were once again raised over the city. In all, Tucson had been occupied by the Confederate forces for eighty days.

STICK 'EM UP

THE OLD WEST AROUND TUCSON

Tombstone Made Famous

Founded in 1877, Tombstone is located a little over an hour's drive from downtown Tucson and is often visited by visitors and Tucson residents. It's the Old West personified to its ardent fans.

Prospector Ed Schieffelin, staying in what was then Camp Huachuca, inadvertently became Tombstone's father. He would often venture out on his own, despite warnings that he would encounter Apaches along the way, and was often told that the only thing he'd find prospecting would be his own "tombstone." Despite these dire predictions, he managed to find a silver mine of his own, and he even named it Tombstone as a nod to the naysayers. By 1879, the town had been laid out and new residents had begun to pour in. This included gunmen, homesteaders, women of the night and other prospectors. By 1881, Tombstone had a population numbering between four and five thousand residents and quickly became one of the wealthiest mining towns in the Southwest. By the late 1890s, the town had peaked at about fifteen thousand residents.

The town was like any other in the Southwest. Little would be remembered about Tombstone were it not for the gun battle that rattled the windows and raised the blood pressure on October 26, 1881. The famed Gunfight at the OK Corral lasted only a handful of seconds but would be forever remembered in connection to the town. Tombstone's nickname became "the Town Too Tough to Die."

Pictured is Wyatt Earp (*seated second from the left, with a hand on his shoulder*) when he served on the Dodge City Peace Commission in June 1883. *Standing, from left to right*: W.H. Harris, Luke Short and Bat Masterson. *Seated, left to right*: Charlie Bassett, Earp, Frank McLain and Neal Brown. *From* Photographs of the American West, 1861–1912.

On that fateful day, Wyatt, Virgil and Morgan Earp, not to mention Doc Holliday, exchanged a hail of bullets with Billy Clanton and his pals, "the Cowboys," Frank and Tom McLaury. The Clanton and McLaury families worked on a nearby cattle ranch and often moonlighted their services for extra cash. They weren't above much when it came to their side hustles, not even murder. They'd run afoul of the Earps and Holliday the day before the shootout as a matter of fact, just as the outlaws came into Tombstone for supplies. The Earps essentially formed the law enforcement side of the battle. With their prior run-in on the minds of everyone present, the two bands came face to face in a vacant lot, just behind the corral, at the end of Fremont Street at around 3:00 p.m. A shot was fired, although which side fired that first round is open to debate, and the historic battle began. Virgil Earp, according to accounts, fired a shot into Billy Clanton's chest. Holliday, they say, let off a shotgun blast that hit Tom McLaury in the chest. More than thirty rounds were fired in about thirty seconds. When the dust settled, the McLaury brothers and Clanton were dead. Their two accomplices, Ike Clanton and Billy Claiborne, fled on foot. Doc Holliday and Virgil and Morgan Earp were also wounded.

Today, Tombstone is a popular tourist attraction for historians and fans of cowboy lore. The city features the corral, which is still standing, and reenactments full of cowboys and simulated gunfire, plus the famed Boothill Cemetery just down the road and a number old-time saloons.

TRAIN ROBBERIES

A mail train rattled through the Tucson area, kicking up dust and scaring the lizards, in an area today known as Vail—a trip like many that came before it, only this time history would be watching. Back in 1887, although some claim it was three years earlier, the area was just another bleak desert landscape, another gap between the growing number of cities popping up throughout the American Southwest. Train operators little realized how that particular trip would differ from the hundreds of other runs through the heat and dust. Why would they? Someone would have to be crazy to be out there battling rattlers and scorpions in the heat.

Nonetheless, that train soon found itself stopped on railroad tracks that had been blown to pieces and then shot full of lead. A group of masked outlaws quickly surrounded the train and made off with gold and cash in mere minutes. This was the group's second train robbery as well, which meant that the gang now had a hefty sum in its possession.

Not long after the robberies, due to the severity of the crime and the large haul of stolen mail bags, estimated at about $72,000, a posse led by Sheriff Bob Leatherwood dashed into the desert to track them down. They followed the robbers to a spot in Colossal Cave Mountain Park roughly twenty miles outside of Tucson. Back then, the hideout was known only as the Five-Mile Cave. The robbers were there, hiding out somewhere in the system of caverns, but the posse saw neither hide nor hair of them. After searching the area as best they could, the lawmen moved on, giving the outlaws a chance to escape. Like most tales of the Old West, more than one version of this story exists. Contrasting tales of the robbery say that Leatherwood faced gunfire when he attempted to go into the cave. It's said that he sat outside for two weeks waiting for them to leave, only to learn that they'd taken a secret back way out.

It's rumored that much of their loot was abandoned in the caves, however, lost to time somewhere in the forty miles of underworld. Now the cave is a national park, close cousin to the more-famous Kartchner Caverns, and features daily tours by park staff, many of whom will share the story of the bandits' lost treasure. Variations of the story hold that the men were all killed, save bandit Phil Carver, in a gunfight between the posse and the crooks that took place inside a saloon shortly after their escape. Carver alone survived and was eventually sentenced to eighteen years in prison. Upon his release, with Leatherwood still sheriff, Carver made his way to Tucson. There he was watched until, one day, he evaded his pursuers and made his way back to the cave. When Leatherwood's men caught his trail, they found only empty, dug-up mail bags…and no sign of Carver or the loot.

While parts of the story have been verified through historical records, other details seem lost to history, leading the true story of Tucson's bank robbers to be nothing more than a cowboy legend.

TUCSON OPERA HOUSE BURNS

NO CASUALTIES IN 1930 CONFLAGRATION

Fire is a common occurrence in the southwestern states, although they aren't often caused by exploding film. Yet this is exactly what happened at the Tucson Opera House, once located downtown along East Congress Avenue. The fire erupted in May 1918 with at least three hundred people packed into the building at the time. Theatergoers were preparing to watch the film *The Modern Musketeers* when there was a loud *bang* and the screen went blank.

Someone yelled "Fire!"

The blaze began in the control room, known as the operating room, shortly after 8:00 p.m. and right after a comedy film finished. An experienced operator, H.K. Monroe, managed to extinguish the fire in the room but failed to stop flames from shooting up the ventilator, where they began to burn the roof. The roof, made of tar paper, quickly burst into flames.

The initial call for the patrons to flee was met with a second call to remain calm, to avoid a panicked rush for the exits. Two individuals, Charles Sipp and R.D. Carpenter, urged the crowd to move slowly and to wait until the exit doors were opened before making their way outside. Walter Burroughs, the opera house's organist, played until most had left the theater. These safety measures are largely credited with preventing any deaths as a result of the fire. A few stragglers, meanwhile, had made their way to the stage to observe the flames above them.

By this time, many had left the building, and the fire had spread to the grill directly above the auditorium. The lightwork hung above the grill assembly,

A parade passes the Tucson Opera House in 1887. The parade traveled down Pennington Street. Behind the parade, the Pima County Courthouse can also be seen. *From the* Tucson Citizen.

which was made of wood, and quickly ignited. Those patrons who remained to observe the fire above them were ordered to leave the building as well. Moments later, the flames chewed through the remaining wood, and the entire assembly collapsed in a ball of smoke and flame into the theater. The large theater curtains and more also fell into the auditorium, by now bathed in fire. Within moments, the seats were also ablaze. The opera house fire, it was later said, could be seen as far away as the San Xavier Mission.

Fire crews worked diligently to battle the fire and pulled hoses from a number of hydrants, called plugs, to reach the building. Hoses were pulled from Stone Avenue and Congress, as well as from Pennington Street, according to news accounts. As crews worked to extinguish the blaze, volunteers rushed inside to save as much of the furniture as they could. People on the ground soon began to fear that the entire block would go up. Thousands watched the blaze, according to accounts. Injuries were thankfully slight, reports indicated. Monroe suffered singed hair, and a woman who had escaped the building nearly fainted outside.

Power was shut off to the block, and phone lines were disconnected as fire crews poured water over the blaze, through the roof and into the theater, over the walls and through doorways. Police and even the mayor helped coordinate the extinguishing effort in the darkness, keeping the burning flames in check within the opera house. This coordinated act helped keep the rest of the block from destruction. They battled the blaze and won in just over one hour.

A.V. Grossetta, owner of the opera house that he built in 1897, stated the following day that he would rebuild the house, but as a motion picture company for the Broadway Theater Company. He had no plans to keep the stage. Local business owners, thankful for the quick response to the fire, collected money to send to the fire department. In total, they presented $129 and a box of cigars to the department as thanks. Grossetta, meanwhile, estimated that it would cost $15,000 to replace the building before opening up again. Total damages were thought to be around $30,000. Plans went into effect to reopen the theater by the fall, when a group of Tucson residents were expected back in town from their summer retreats. By September, they had screened their first film, *Riders of the Purple Sage.*

The theater later became the State Theater and closed in the early 1950s for good. The last film played there was the 1951 science fiction classic *When Worlds Collide.*

LIVES LOST IN THE LINE OF DUTY

"End of watch." It's a phrase we hear often, and for the men and women of law enforcement, it holds a deeper and more emotional meaning. The phrase is largely reserved for officers killed in the line of duty—those who paid the ultimate price while protecting the thin blue line—and honors their memory by reflecting on the date that price came due.

That thin blue line, considered the line where bedlam and anarchy meets order and civilization, is guarded by those in law enforcement. While many in law enforcement no longer wear blue, it was the predominant uniform color at the time the term was first coined. It's believed that the term was first used around 1950 by the Los Angeles Police Department. It is symbolized with a black rectangle—running from left to right at the center of a blue band. Variations have been made to this simple symbol over the years, although the meaning remains.

William Elliott

Having only been on the force for a few months, Tucson police officer William Elliott strolled through the Barrio Libre section of downtown on routine foot patrol. It was past midnight on a typical hot July evening. On that day, July 2, 1892, Elliott likely thought that any possible excitement was

Left: Among the monuments to fallen officers at the Tucson Police Department is this sculpture honoring the city's Old West roots. *Author's collection.*

Right: Pictured is Tucson police officer William Elliott, who was the first officer to be killed in the line of duty. He was murdered on July 2, 1892. *Tucson Police Department.*

behind him for this particular shift and that he'd soon be home with his wife and two children. He was wrong—minutes later, Elliott would become the first Tucson police officer to die in the line of duty.

While on Meyer Avenue, between McCormick and Cushing Street, Elliott spotted a notorious criminal, Santos Alvarado, who'd just arrived in Tucson from Phoenix. Alvarado was well known in the Southwest for his sinister deeds and wasn't about to let a single officer on foot take him in. When Elliott spotted him, right in front of Tucson mayor Frederick Maish's residence, he drew his gun to stop the man. His firearm cracked into the sky, the report drawing a few onlookers to the scene. The shot above Alvarado's head did little to diffuse the situation, however, according to those who gathered at the scene. Witnesses to the confrontation included the mayor, who was roused from his sleep by the gunshot.

Two witnesses later said that Alvarado shouted to Elliott, "Shoot me if you want to, you can't arrest me." Alvarado drew a knife. He charged the young officer, plunging his knife into Elliott's heart, but he himself would also suffer a mortal wound. Before his last gasp, the officer managed to get off another shot, killing Alvarado. While both men lay dying, Mayor Maish went to Elliott's aid, but it was too late.

The young father and husband died in the mayor's arms.

William Katzenstein

A handful of years would pass before the second police officer would fall in the line of duty, and oddly enough, he shared the same first name as Officer Elliott. He died in the month of July as well, just as Elliott had. William Katzenstein had a wife and young daughter.

His end of watch came on July 26, 1902, when he responded to a fire between the hours of 11:00 p.m. and midnight. The fire was reported at a local business on South Meyer Avenue near Broadway Boulevard. Katzenstein, on patrol nearby, responded quickly to the scene.

Unbeknownst to him, someone was keeping a close watch on his patrol. Theodoro Elias had been stalking the officer for five weeks or more, ever since Katzenstein arrested a close friend of his. Elias seethed with anger over the incident and had promised friends on that hot July evening that his enemy, Katzenstein, would be dead before the end of the night. The structure fire presented to him the perfect opportunity.

While protecting the business from those with a mind to grab a few things from the store while no one was looking, Katzenstein soon decided to help combat the conflagration himself. Besides being a policeman, he also served Tucson as the assistant fire chief. While serving in the latter capacity, Katzenstein opted to remove his sidearm. He left the gun with a clerk at another nearby business and rushed back to the fiery scene.

As Katzenstein worked to open a fireplug, Elias saw his chance. He'd seen the officer hand over his gun and knew there would never be a better chance to mete out his vengeance. Elias drew his weapon and fired a shot. The bullet grazed the officer's ear but only knocked Katzenstein off his feet. Confused, the policeman got back to his feet and was shot again. This time Elias put a bullet into the officer's head just under his right eye. A doctor who happened to be on the scene rushed to help, but it was too late for Katzenstein. He died after serving two years on the force, leaving his wife and daughter behind.

Elias was chased from the scene and caught on the steps of the courthouse.

ROBERT CUMMINS

More than thirty years would pass before the next officer-related death in the city. On September 7, 1936, Tucson Motorcycle Patrol officer Robert Cummins traveled with a number of colleagues to Phoenix, where they served as parade escorts for an American League convention. Cummins had served ten years with the Border Patrol before taking a job with the Tucson Police Department. He'd been on the force nine months. Tragedy struck the parade group as the officers set out to return to Tucson. At the intersection of Van Buren and Sixteenth, the officer's motorcycle careened wildly over loose gravel. Cummins suffered serious injuries when his motorcycle crashed.

After he was transported to a nearby hospital, reports indicated that Cummins regained consciousness only once after the crash. He recognized his wife, according to firsthand accounts, but then lapsed into a coma. He succumbed to his injuries four days later. He was survived by his wife and four children.

Tucson police officers not on duty, along with the Tucson chief of police, escorted his body from Phoenix to Tucson for burial.

BARRY HEADRICKS

Working narcotics is no easy task, even for the best of cops. It can be a brutal and trying part of law enforcement. It can even prove deadly. Five-year police veteran Barry Headricks was one of those tough cops. He had been assigned to the Metropolitan Area Narcotics Squad for just over a year before his end of watch came on October 28, 1974.

Headricks found himself that fateful day inside a second-floor home of the Colony Apartments on Eighth Street. He'd made all the preparations leading up to that meeting and found himself in the apartment with two ounces of heroin. Excusing himself briefly, he went out to check the authenticity of the merchandise. He returned five minutes later when it was confirmed that the heroin was real—only he didn't go alone. He came back with nine agents and the deputy county attorney. Headricks and the others intended to conduct a search based on probable cause, but things wouldn't go as planned.

After they broke through the door, two suspects fled into a bedroom. They slammed the door behind them, although it didn't slow Headricks down

A pedestal outside the Tucson Police Department's downtown location honors officers who lost their lives in the line of duty. *Author's collection.*

for long. He crashed through the door just as one of the suspects, Rufus Mincey, fired a pistol at him. Headricks was struck but managed to fire back, hitting both of the suspects. Although fellow officers hurried him to a nearby hospital, the five-year veteran passed away within an hour.

Headricks was survived by his parents and a sister.

JAMES SMITH

Tucson's Speedway Boulevard is one of those roads that sees a lot of action. Nearly every day, in fact, there's a crash, a breakdown, horns blaring or an altercation of some kind. While the road has changed since the 1980s, it's always been a busy place, particularly in the mornings and early evenings. Motorcycle officer James Smith, days before Halloween on October 28, 1980, responded to just such a crash and was near the Plumer Avenue intersection in the middle lane when a station wagon clipped him. The vehicle was changing lanes, despite Smith's sirens and lights. The minor hit threw Smith from his motorcycle and into the lane of oncoming traffic, where he was struck by another vehicle.

Smith, a married father of two, died at the scene. He was a four-year veteran of the police force and served in the U.S. Air Force prior to becoming a police officer.

JEFFREY ROSS

Less than two years later, Tucson would mourn the loss of another officer when four-year police veteran Jeffrey Ross was killed in a shooting. Ross worked the Metro Area Narcotics squad, and on the evening of February 18, 1982, he and other officers entered the Ranch House Bar on Casa Grande Highway to arrest Clifford Hamilton. Hamilton, the manager of the bar, faced not just Ross but also a group of officers determined to bring him in. Armed, Hamilton tried in vain to escape by firing at the oncoming officers when they entered a room at the back of the business. He fired only a single round, hitting Ross in the chest. The other officers present returned fire before Hamilton could react. Hamilton was killed immediately. Ross, who was rushed to an emergency medical center, died from his injuries seventeen minutes later. He was survived by his wife.

PATRICK K. HARDESTY

Patrick Hardesty, a twenty-year veteran with the U.S. Marine Corps, became the next officer to lose his life in the line of duty. The married father of three responded to a hit-and-run on Memorial Day 2003. While investigating the incident, the officer responded to a residence on Fort Lowell Road in search of a man suspected of being involved, Juan Montenegro-Cruz. Hardesty reportedly made contact with the subject, but Cruz escaped while Hardesty tried to ascertain his identity. A foot chase ensued in which Hardesty dogged the suspect through the backyards of nearby residences. Another officer, assisting in the investigation, heard Hardesty radio in the pursuit while he interviewed other subjects inside the residence. The assisting officer joined in the pursuit and found Cruz. He detained the man pending further investigation, while other responding officers searched for Hardesty. The officer was found in a nearby backyard, where he'd been shot three times. He later died in the hospital.

Hardesty served as a reserve police officer for twelve years. He'd worked as a full-time officer for only one year before he was killed. He was survived by three children and his wife.

ERIK HITE

Sunday, June 1, 2008, started out as any other day, although that peace was shattered by gunfire just after 10:00 a.m. Police were quick to respond to the incident, and by 10:22 a.m., they were in pursuit of the suspect vehicle. Reports flooded in of the incident, in which an unknown suspect fired a rifle at two homes outside the city limits. As Pima County sheriff's deputies dashed to the scene, they discovered that the suspect, Nick Delich, had sped from the scene in his vehicle. He opened fire on the officers from his car, at which point they engaged in pursuit; the first deputy to respond was wounded.

Not long after, Tucson officers joined the chase and spotted Delich's vehicle. They joined the pursuit but found themselves under attack when Delich opened fire on them as well. The vehicle sped around the corner of Tanque Verde and Tomahawk Trail, and there he waited, prepared to ambush anyone who drove around the corner. Erik D. Hite, a twenty-one-year U.S. Air Force veteran, turned the blind corner first and faced the full brunt of the attack alone. His vehicle was struck several times. One round hit Hite. After firing at the officer, Delich fled once again and was eventually apprehended, although not without first getting off another shot and hitting a sheriff's deputy. Hite was transported to the hospital after Delich surrendered but succumbed to his gunshot wound the next day.

Hite was survived by his wife and two children. He'd served the Tucson Police Department for four years. His widow, Nohemy Hite, founded a daycare in his name three years after his death. The facility opened in 2012 to parents who work in law enforcement and other similar agencies. It can be found online at erikhitefoundation.org.

PUBLICLY KILLED

EXECUTIONS IN FLORENCE

One hundred individuals have been executed in the state of Arizona since 1910. Only one of those killed has been a woman. Eva Dugan was put to the gallows in 1930 for the crime of murder. According to statistics from the Arizona Department of Corrections, Rehabilitation and Reentry, twenty-eight of those individuals were killed by the hangman's noose. Thirty-seven died from inhaling lethal gas, with the remaining thirty-five killed by a lethal chemical cocktail injected into their bloodstreams.

Death sentences have been a regular fixture for Florence State Prison, found just north of Tucson, since it was constructed in the early 1900s. Executions at the prison have been carried out since 1910. The ultimate price has been suspended twice, however, sparing the lives of those who committed first-degree murder in favor of a life behind bars—for some a fate worse than death. The first suspension began on December 8, 1916, following a new measure eliminating the act as a form of punishment for those convicted of first-degree murder. Nearly two years later, that measure was stricken. On December 5, 1918, the penalty of death was once again restored to the justice system. This time, it would hold until April 1962, after which no one would be put to death by the state for thirty years. In April 1992, the penalty was once again reinstated.

Florence State Prison, also known as Arizona State Prison Complex–Florence, conducted its early executions on scaffolding one floor above the cells found on death row. Crews built a trapdoor that dropped open during an execution so the body would dangle above the floor below. Jose Lopez

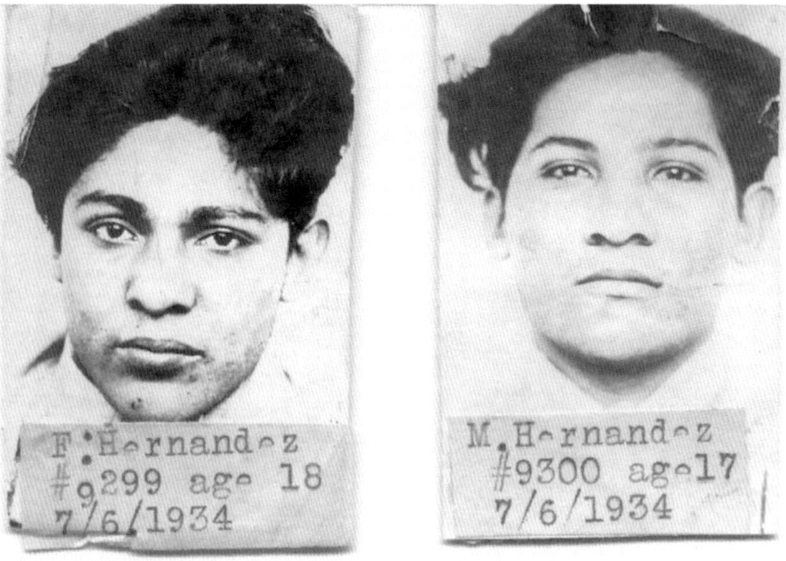

Pictured are Fred and Manuel Hernandez. The two brothers were the first convicts in Arizona to be put to death by lethal gas. They were killed on July 6, 1934, at 5:00 a.m. *Arizona Historical Society.*

was the first to be hanged under the death penalty in the state of Arizona. He was killed on January 5, 1910.

Lopez was accused of murdering Maria Espinoza, a mother of seven. Espinoza had argued with Lopez earlier in the day over a matter of $8 owed to Lopez's father. According to inflation calculators, that would be the equivalent of just over $200 in the year 2020. When Lopez failed to pay the amount owed her father, Lopez left her residence and later returned with a shotgun. It's said that one of her children, upon hearing Lopez enter the home, confronted him.

"What are you doing with that shotgun?" he asked the man, according to accounts of the murder. This would not stop the angry Lopez from murdering Espinoza.

Lopez met swift justice for his heinous act, as he was put to death just over five months later. Two other death row inmates would follow in his footsteps that year, Cesario Sanchez and Rafael Barela, both of whom were sent to the gallows in December of that year.

Following the terrible events of Eva Dugan's demise (featured in the next chapter), the State of Arizona opted to find a more humane way to end the lives of its death row inmates: lethal gas. Manuel and Fred

Hernandez, two brothers, were the first to be put to death by lethal gas the morning of July 6, 1934. They were killed at 5:00 a.m. The brothers, seventeen and eighteen years old, were convicted of robbing a Casa Grande miner in January 1933. The two hit Charles T. Washburn on the head and, thinking him dead, carried him to a nearby well to dispose of the body. They realized to their dismay that Washburn had not died from the blow, however. Not to be deterred, they finished him off with a double-barreled shotgun before dumping him in. Roughly one year later, they paid the ultimate price for their crime.

Following a thirty-year absence, Arizona's death penalty resumed in 1992, when Donald E. Harding was put to death in April of that year by lethal gas. The last man to die by lethal gas prior to Harding's death was Manuel E. Silvas, who died from lethal gas in 1963. Oddly enough, despite the state's switch to lethal injection in 1993, one more sentence of death would be carried out by lethal gas. Walter Burnhart LaGrand was the last to die by this measure on March 3, 1999, at 9:30 p.m. The German national was the last in the country to die by this means. He'd been convicted with his brother, Karl Heinz, after the two killed a man in an armed robbery attempt in 1982.

Years earlier, John George Brewer became the first inmate to die by lethal injection. He was put to death on March 3 as well, like LaGrand, but in the year 1993. Brewer was convicted of strangling his girlfriend, Rita Brier, in 1987. She was twenty-two weeks pregnant at the time of her death. Brewer never asked to be spared the death penalty and, according to reports, admitted that he deserved it. His last meal consisted of a number of items, including pork chops, bacon, shrimp, applesauce, coffee with cream and sugar and more.

Joseph Wood was the last to be put to death as of January 2020. He died by lethal injection on July 23, 2014, at 3:49 p.m. Wood was sentenced to death in 1991 following a series of murders in August 1989 in which he killed Debbie Dietz, twenty-nine, and Gene Dietz, fifty-five, in the family's body shop. Wood had dated Debbie on and off for five years in what was described as a turbulent relationship. When police responded to the incident and attempted to detain Wood, he fought back by reaching for his gun, but only after he had placed it on the ground in apparent submission. He pointed the weapon at police, who responded swiftly by shooting him several times. Wood was not killed, however, and underwent extensive surgery following the incident. For his last meal, he requested only two cookies.

Wood was administered a lethal cocktail of midazolam and hydromorphone, and his death was expected to follow within ten minutes. This wasn't the case, however. The drugs were administered, but death did not come quickly. For two hours, he snorted and gasped for air, according to reports, until the injection finally achieved its purpose. His death prompted a review of death penalty measures in the state, although a total of 117 inmates remained on death row as of January 2020.

THE FIRST FEMALE EXECUTION

THE STORY OF EVA DUGAN'S DEMISE

It was a dark February morning when Eva Dugan walked, unaided, to her own death. At 5:01 a.m., she stepped up to the top of the gallows and remained silent when asked if she had any last words. The trap, sprung by an unknown handler, dropped open beneath her feet. She was pronounced dead a minute later at 5:02 a.m., February 21, 1930. At that moment, she went down in history as the first woman to be executed in the state of Arizona.

Dugan's sordid tale began years earlier in 1927, when she went to work at a ranch in Pima County near Tucson. She moved to Arizona after working as a cabaret singer in Alaska, where she'd gone during the Klondike Gold Rush. In Arizona, she worked as a housekeeper for chicken rancher Andrew J. Mathis. She didn't last long in the new position, however, although the reason why Mathis fired her is unclear. Mathis himself disappeared around that time.

Authorities were quickly put on Dugan's scent, as she reportedly tried to sell some of the rancher's belongings to neighbors around the time of his disappearance. Besides the man himself, his cash box, belongings and his vehicle (a Dodge Coupe) were also missing. During the investigation, it was discovered that Eva had been married five times and that each time her husband had gone missing. With the search on, it was only a matter of time before authorities got their hands on her. A postal worker in White Plains, New York, is credited with recognizing Dugan when she sent a postcard to her father. She was soon apprehended and sent back to face her accusers in Arizona. It was discovered that Dugan had been in possession of the missing Dodge Coupe and sold it for $600 in Kansas City, Missouri. She was, in fact, charged only with auto theft at the time, but that changed when a camper came across Mathis's decomposed remains. She was convicted of murdering the elderly man with an axe. Critics of the trial claimed that she was convicted on largely circumstantial evidence and worked for two years to appeal the conviction. Her story gained worldwide attention, and Dugan's casual demeanor earned her the nickname "Cheerful Eva" in a 1930 article in *TIME* magazine.

Upon her conviction, Dugan told jurors, "I'll die with my boots on, an' in full health. An' that's more'n most of you old coots'll be able to boast on."

The mystery of the man named "Jack" remains an intriguing chapter to Dugan's tale. According to Dugan, Jack was hired on as a ranch hand but quickly got into a scuffle with Mathis. The elderly property owner died as a result of that fight. Dugan claimed that she and Jack buried the body together but insisted that he was the one who murdered Mathis. There are some who believe that the mysterious Jack was, in fact, convicted child murderer Edward Hickman, while others believe that Jack never truly existed and was only a figment of Dugan's imagination.

Leading up to her execution, Dugan kept herself busy with knitting. She embroidered handkerchiefs, which she sold to anyone interested in owning one, allegedly to pay for her own coffin. She also made a "jazz dress" from silk and beads, which she planned to wear to her hanging before changing her mind. It's believed that she was buried in the dress instead. She also spoke to the media during her incarceration, charging one dollar for every interview she gave.

Her death remains a morbid tale, however, not simply because she was the first woman to be put to death in the state, but due to the grisly manner in which she was hanged. The morning began as normally as possible considering an execution was looming. A group of twelve reporters was allowed a chance to visit with Dugan an hour before the scheduled execution. While understandably awkward, Dugan shook the hands of her visitors and told them that she would walk to the gallows without assistance, but she did request someone go with her. The *Arizona Daily Star* reported in its February 21, 1930 edition that her voice quavered slightly when she spoke, but she otherwise showed no other sign of emotion.

A last-minute effort with the Prison and Parole Board to stay the execution had been denied by this point, and Dugan said her farewells to those present before walking silently to her demise. After the trap opened

A 1930s postcard offers a view of the prison in Florence, just north of Tucson, where many convicted felons have been sent after being sentenced to death. *Online Archive of California.*

and she dropped, reporters and other spectators witnessed a grotesque scene. The noose severed her head from her body, which dropped into a dark pool of blood to the floor. Her head rolled to a corner of the room. Dugan was fifty-two.

Her gruesome demise rattled those present, for a decapitation to occur during a hanging was a rare occurrence, let alone for the first woman executed. It was soon revealed that Eva herself was hesitant to meet the noose, as searchers reported that they found four razor blades in the waist of her pants the morning of her death. A further search unearthed a bottle of poison in her cell, although why she never used the blades or the poison remains a mystery. It's possible that the prison guards discovered her plans before she could act on them.

The Florence State Prison warden announced that he would never reveal who operated the trapdoor that led to Dugan's death and that plans were underway to bury her in the prison graveyard located outside the prison walls.

Her grisly death—the first to allow women to witness an execution in the state—helped change execution practices. Only two others would be hanged after her: Refugio Macias on March 7, 1930, and Herbert Young on August 21, 1931. By 1934, the hangman's noose had been replaced by death in a gas chamber. In 1993, executions by lethal injection replaced gas. The injection uses a mix of drugs to knock the patient unconscious, stop their breathing and create heart arrhythmia, which causes an irregular heartbeat. The practice is still used in many states.

The noose used to hang Eva was displayed at the Pinal County Historic Society and Museum in Florence, Arizona, as an interesting relic of a tragic and coldhearted series of events.

TUCSON'S SPANISH FLU

HOW THE 1918 PANDEMIC AFFECTED THE CITY

While 2020 proved to be the year of the deadly coronavirus pandemic across the globe, the world faced a deadly flu bug more than a century before. That strain, which came to be known as the Spanish influenza outbreak of 1918, infected an estimated 500 million people and caused nearly 50 million deaths worldwide, according to numbers from the Centers for Disease Control and Prevention (CDC). About 675,000 deaths were believed to have resulted from the Spanish influenza in the United States between 1918 and 1919. It's believed that this strain of flu had avian origins.

The strain is thought to have originated in America from U.S. military personnel and was particularly deadly, even among healthy individuals, during a period when antibiotics were not readily available to treat infections that resulted from the illness. Vaccines were also not available for treatment in 1918, according to the CDC. As a result of the pandemic, the average life expectancy of Americans was lowered by twelve years. The pandemic was thought to be made worse when soldiers, returning home from World War I, were packed into ships for their return voyage, creating a new wave of infection. More people ultimately died as a result of the pandemic than died in the war itself. The war, however, did lead to a shortage in medical personnel in the United States, as many were overseas when the pandemic began to ripple across the globe.

The Spanish flu, named for the location where news of the pandemic was originally reported and not where it began, attacked the world in three waves,

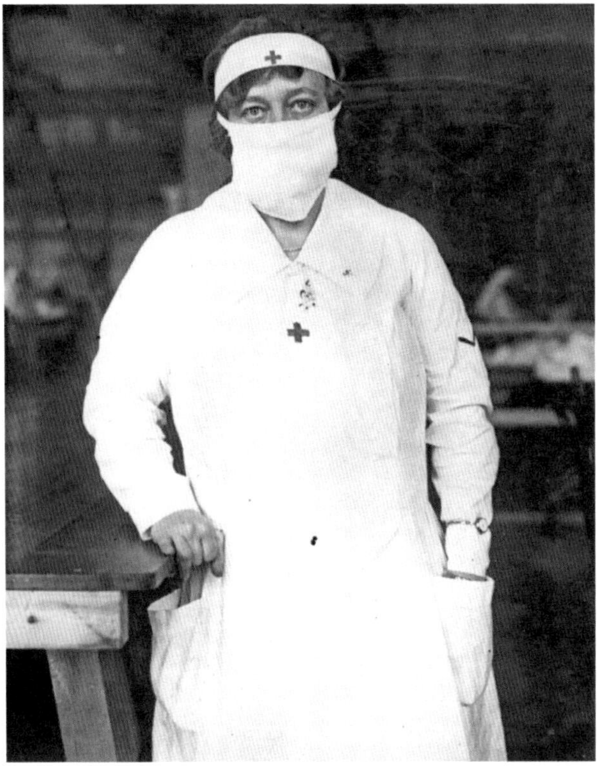

A Red Cross nurse can be seen wearing a gauze mask in this photograph taken in 1918. More than one hundred years later, masks would become commonplace once again. *National Archives and Records Administration.*

according to historical graphs. The first began in March 1918. The second and strongest wave came in the fall of that year. The third and final wave appeared in the summer of 1919. The most lethal wave, which accounted for most of the deaths in the United States, came in the fall of 1918.

Tucson, like every other city in the United States, also suffered losses as a result of the pandemic. When the flu began marching across the nation like an invisible wildfire, Tucson residents numbered only about 20,000, a much smaller number than the 980,263 seen today throughout the metropolitan area. The city itself only covered eight square miles. According to the *Arizona Daily Star*, deaths were attributed to influenza before the Spanish flu had even been named. Tucson's outbreak is believed to have begun in the spring of 1918. Hundreds of residents died locally, while, statewide, it was estimated the flu killed about 1 percent of Arizona's total population that year. The highest number of deaths occurred between October 1918 and January 1919, where death certificates from that period showed a spike in deaths, particularly with younger people, from bronchial pneumonia. While death certificates weren't issued for everyone back then, estimates indicate that at least 300 died in Tucson, although the number is generally believed to be higher. The average age of those said to have died from the flu was twenty-five years old. Most were sick for at least a week before succumbing to the illness.

Tucson newspapers first reported cases in both Winslow and Flagstaff in early October 1918. Two hundred cases were reported in Winslow and sixty in Flagstaff in the October 4, 1918 edition of the *Arizona Daily Star*. By October 10, 1918, the newspaper was reporting more than twenty cases in Tucson.

The deadly outbreak caused acting mayor of Tucson A.C. Bernard to close schools, movie theaters (known then as motion picture houses), pool halls, churches and "places of amusement where people congregate." Newspapers covered the Spanish flu extensively, with a particular focus on how to prevent spreading the disease, advertisements for cure-alls and news on the deaths of notables who died from the influenza strain. By October 1918, masks were required clothing throughout the city, to be worn in all buildings and even while out on the streets within the city limits, leading to June 1919, when deaths related to the outbreak began to fade. Despite the risk of a ten-dollar fine, not a small sum in those days, many Tucson residents opted not to wear masks, according to newspaper reports.

TUCSONANS AND WORLD WAR II

THE DEATH OF JAMES VAN HORN ABOARD THE *ARIZONA*

December 1941 is a date that's hard to miss, particularly for historians and soldiers of every stripe, not to mention their descendants. Sunday, December 7, precipitated the United States' entry into World War II, as Japan launched an assault on the Pearl Harbor Naval Base in Honolulu, Hawaii, at approximately 8:00 a.m. The sneak attack left more than 2,400 Americans dead as a result, sank twenty navy vessels and obliterated three hundred airplanes. The following day, President Franklin D. Roosevelt sought Congressional approval for a declaration of war against Japan. While Great Britain and France entered the war in 1939, the United States had not officially joined the effort against the coalition of Adolf Hitler's Germany, Italy and Japan. That changed after Pearl Harbor.

World War II would continue for six long years, leaving anywhere between 45 to 60 million people dead, including the 6 million Jews who were killed in Nazi concentration camps. Germany formally surrendered on May 8, 1945. After the United States dropped atomic bombs on both Nagasaki and Hiroshima, the Japanese surrendered in August. The terrible, deadly conflict had finally come to an end.

When it came to Pearl Harbor, military minds believed that the naval base was too far away from Japan for it to attack there. Japan was nearly four thousand miles away after all. It would be folly for the country to rain death and destruction at such a distant target when the islands in the South Pacific presented a much closer objective. As a result, the Hawaiian base was left

The USS *Arizona* burns in this 1941 photograph taken during the attack on Pearl Harbor before sinking to the bottom of the harbor, where it remains to this day. *National Archives and Records Administration.*

virtually undefended and a tasty target for their enemies. The Pacific Fleet, nearly all of it, was moored at the base.

This included the USS *Arizona*, which was hit ten minutes after the 8:00 a.m. attack began. Japanese fighters dropped a 1,800-pound bomb onto the battleship that went through the upper deck and came to rest in the *Arizona*'s forward ammunition magazines before it detonated. The subsequent explosion devastated the ship, and it quickly sank with more than one thousand souls aboard. The surprise morning attack came to an end two hours after it began, with every ship in the fleet damaged or destroyed.

While most of the ships were salvaged and put back into service, two were not. The USS *Arizona* and the USS *Utah* could not be saved. "Yesterday, December 7, 1941—a date which will live in infamy—the United States of America was suddenly and deliberately attacked by naval and air forces of the Empire of Japan," said Roosevelt to a joint session of Congress. Two years after the beginning of World War II, the United States had officially entered the fray.

Originally manufactured in 1916, the USS *Arizona* weighed a whopping 31,400 tons when it was built at the New York Naval Yard in Brooklyn. The battleship went through a major upgrade by the 1930s, complete with improved armaments. Prior to Pearl Harbor, the *Arizona* was notable for having transported President Herbert Hoover to Puerto Rico and the Virgin Islands. By 1940, it was stationed at Pearl Harbor, its final resting place. The battleship was left at the bottom of the harbor, the dead entombed within, and became a memorial in the 1950s. By the 1960s, a shrine had been erected over what remained of the vessel. Today, the USS *Arizona* Memorial is operated by the National Park Service and is a frequent stop for visitors to the area.

In 2016, construction began on the USS *Arizona* Mall Memorial near the University of Arizona campus in Tucson. Work ended in time for a dedication on Sunday, December 4, 2016, to commemorate the seventy-fifth anniversary of the attack on Pearl Harbor. The west end of the University of Arizona Mall matches the rough size and shape of the historic battleship. An outline of the ship can be found on the grounds, as can 1,177 medallions, one for each of the men who died aboard the ship. The site, designed by David Carter, is located on East University Boulevard in Tucson.

Tucson's connection to the famed battleship is a young man named James Van Horn. Van Horn, a student at Tucson High School in 1941, had just turned seventeen when he made the decision to quit school and enlist in the U.S. Navy. Before the year came to a close, he would be among those entombed in the USS *Arizona*. Van Horn's medallion can be found at the USS *Arizona* Mall Memorial. Van Horn was survived by his mother, Mrs. Bonnie F. Cope, according to military records. After his death, Van Horn was awarded the Purple Heart, the American Defense Service Medal with Fleet Clasp, the Asiatic-Pacific Campaign Medal with Star and the World War II Victory Medal. In 1958, as fundraising efforts were underway to build the memorial shrine at Pearl Harbor, Tucson mayor Don Hummel declared December 1, 1958, to be James Van Horn Day in Tucson. His mother received a copper plaque designating the special day to honor her son's service to the country.

"I hope the memorial can be built over the ship. I feel that we all have a special cause in a memorial to those who are still buried in the ship," Mrs. Cope said during a newspaper interview at the time.

BOMBER CRASH

DEATH OVER PANTANO WASH

It was a cool November morning in the skies over Tucson. The Thanksgiving holiday sat firmly in the rear-view mirror, and the Christmas holiday lay just ahead. World War II was well underway, with D-Day having occurred months earlier in June, and much of the planet was on edge. For many, the holiday season wouldn't be as festive as other years. In Tucson, the holidays kicked off with a storm of mayhem over the area of Pantano Wash.

The Wash is a portion of Ciénega Creek, an intermittent stream, that connects with the Rillito River. The Wash is now better known for the Pantano River Park, which features paved walkways, restrooms and picnic tables. Over the years, everything from fossils to rusted car bodies have been unearthed along the stretch of land. But in 1944, the area was still relatively quiet compared to the east side residents see today.

Two B-24 Liberators with the 233rd Combat Crew Training Squadron lifted off the tarmac in the early morning hours of November 30, 1944. They departed from what was then known as Davis-Monthan Army Base for a routine training flight north east of Tucson. Tragedy struck at approximately 7:40 a.m. when the two planes collided over Pantano Wash, a large drainage canal that cuts through a portion of the community. The crash occurred midway between East Broadway and East Speedway at an altitude between 1,000 and 1,500 feet, according to an *Arizona Daily Star* article at the time. The planes collided while swinging into a formation flight pattern, and one pilot was blinded by the sun in his face.

The Consolidated B-24 Liberator, which entered service in 1941, measured just over sixty-seven feet in length. *National Museum of the USAF.*

There were no survivors from either bomber—eighteen airmen died in the fiery crash. Original reports indicated that nineteen men perished, although it was quickly discovered that the nineteenth man had been grounded due to a last-minute change of orders. Shortly after the crash, local newspapers shared the names of those killed. Two of the airmen were survived by wives living in Tucson.

The Consolidated B-24 Liberator was one of the most heavily produced bombers of the era and was used throughout World War II in every aspect of war. The bombers were used in Western Europe, Japan and in the South Pacific, particularly due to their ability to carry a heavy arsenal of bombs. Their popularity didn't last long, however, as they were replaced by the larger Boeing B-29 Superfortresses, and other planes, by the end of the war.

The Pantano Wash accident was the worst of its kind from the Tucson air base following the wartime institution of heavy bombardment combat training.

Remains from the crash could still be found decades later, including an intact .50-caliber round found by a group of men with metal detectors, according to a 2017 *Arizona Daily Star* article. One of the members of the Tucson-based metal detector club, who remembered being woken up by the explosive midair collision when he was a teenager, mentioned the horrific

The bridge at Pantano Wash offers a unique feature to those who cross by foot: a plaque honoring those who died in a bomber collision in 1944. *Author's collection.*

incident. After an investigation into the discovery, they found that the round was indeed a long-lost relic from the collision. The club, Detectors Unlimited Inc., actively worked to name a bridge connecting Kolb Road and Sabino Canyon Road after the men who died in service to their country.

A commemorative plaque can now be found on the bridge with the names of the deceased prominently displayed.

FEAR FROM ABOVE

AIRPLANE CRASHES OF TUCSON

While the bomber collision created a grisly sight in the skies over Tucson, the tragedy wasn't the only one of its kind to occur in this part of the Southwest.

On July 8, 1957, just four days after the Independence Day holiday, a pair of F-86 Saberjet Fighters departed from Davis-Monthan Air Force Base on a routine training flight. As they soared high above Tucson over Mount Bigelow, the two crafts crashed into each other. Amazingly, the collision took no lives, as both pilots managed to eject from the jets and avoided serious injury, according to news accounts at the time. One of the Saberjets crash-landed, almost intact, in the Catalina Mountains. The pilot was rescued in the forest nearby. What's left of the jet remains there to this day.

Hikers can see the wreckage while trekking along the Butterfly Trail, part of the Catalina Mountains series of trails. Called the "Wreck Trek," the side jaunt begins at the trailhead and continues for two and a half miles. From the Novio Spring area, turn left where the trail crosses the stream and proceed up a series of steps made from logs. An unmarked trail will veer to the right, where hikers will see the first signs of jet debris.

Ten years after the collision over Mount Bigelow, tragedy struck again, only this time the results were more horrific. Just days before the Christmas holiday on Monday, December 18, 1967, at 5:44 p.m., a U.S. Air Force Phantom Jet plummeted from the air, crashing into a Food Giant grocery

The remains of an F-86 Saberjet Fighter can still be seen in the Catalina Mountains, seen here from the area of Sabino Canyon, more than fifty years later. *Author's collection.*

store and killing four people. The store was located at 1830 South Alvernon. News accounts at the time indicated that it was a miracle more people weren't killed in the crash, as a handful of holiday shoppers were present at the time of the tragedy. Original estimates claimed that at least fifteen were feared dead.

The jet punched into the rear of the store after crashing into a back alley, with a trail of destruction left in its wake. Burning jet fuel created a fiery wave that engulfed a number of homes at the back of the grocery store, killing some of the residents trapped inside. One eyewitness at the time said that the F4D jet created a fireball when it hit the Food Giant. "It exploded like a bomb you see on television," he said.

A December 19, 1967 *Arizona Daily Star* article reported that the jet was based out of Nellis Air Force Base in Nevada and had just taken on sixteen thousand pounds of jet fuel from Davis-Monthan Air Force Base. Witnesses to the incident rushed inside the burning grocery store to help get as many survivors to safety as possible. Estimates indicate that between twenty and thirty people made it out of the building before it was fully engulfed in flames. "It was the worst thing I've ever seen in my life," one witness told reporters. "One minute they were picking greens. The next minute, they just weren't there."

The jet crew was able to parachute to safety prior to the crash. Witnesses said that the plane appeared to be without lights or power when it fell from the sky. Eighty-five firefighters responded to the crash, along with about one hundred law enforcement personnel. Debris from the crash filled five pickup trucks and six dump trucks.

The four victims were later identified as nineteen-year-old Sherry Tilton, thirty-four-year-old Robin Bush, fifty-five-year-old Steffania Palmer and Crystal Siemund (no age given). Damages were estimated at $202,050, which was considered a lot of money in the 1960s. The jet was estimated to cost just over $2 million. Besides destroying the grocery store, two homes and other nearby businesses, the crash also clipped gas lines and caused water main breaks.

The crash is still referred to as one of the worst in Tucson's history. A panel of both military and civilian authorities began an investigation into the deadly crash following the tragedy. Tucson's Mayor James N. Corbett cited a need for an area-wide disaster relief plan.

Fire consumes a number of structures after a U.S. Air Force Phantom Jet crashed into a Food Giant grocery store in 1967. Four people died as a result of the crash. *From the* Arizona Daily Star.

This wouldn't be the last air force jet to crash in the community, however. Twelve years after the Food Giant catastrophe, another jet found itself in trouble. The incident occurred shortly after noon on October 26, 1978, when the A-7D Corsair II jet encountered engine trouble. The pilot aimed the plane toward the University of Arizona (UA) football field before parachuting to safety. While the field would have been an ideal location, the ditched plane never made it to that location. Instead it crashed into a street. One person was killed.

The jet was eight miles from its destination at Davis-Monthan Air Force Base when it stalled. A woman died in her vehicle when the jet plummeted to the street. Her sister, also in the vehicle, suffered third-degree burns over 90 percent of her body. Others were thrown to the ground when the plane crashed. The jets, typically designed to carry twenty thousand pounds of weapons, were not armed during the test flight.

According to newspaper accounts, the pilot ejected from the jet about two hundred feet above the UA campus and suffered only a minor scrape to his ankle. The plane careened onto Highland Street at about two hundred miles per hour, landing on one wing and skidding, creating a fiery wake that destroyed several cars and sent a wall of flame over downtown described as being several stories tall.

The crash also brought down a telephone pole that subsequently cut power to more than two hundred people. The incident brought up concerns of civilian safety near military bases that began after the 1967 jet crash. The 1978 crash didn't ground any jets, however, as eyewitnesses reported that military flights continued over the UA campus while crews still worked to clean up the wreckage on the street.

CASES FROM THE COLD

EXPLORING TUCSON'S UNSOLVED CRIMES

Tucson's long and rich history is one of dedication, perseverance and hard work. As the city is a part of the American Southwest, not to mention its hallowed place as a fixture of the Old West, law enforcement has worked hard to keep its citizens safe. From minor infractions to theft and stone-cold murder, Tucson's residents have counted on that thin blue line to keep them safe. When a crime is committed, it's law enforcement that picks up the pieces to bring justice to the victims. On occasion, however, some crimes prove to be challenging even for the experts.

Across the nation, a number of crimes go unsolved each year. Most unsolved cases, if ten years have passed without any new information, drop into cold case territory. For others, they can drop into the cold case file even sooner should no new evidence materialize. These cases can, however, become active at any time with new testimony, new material evidence or other pertinent new details. At that point, the case can be reopened. Tucson, like any city, has its share of unsolved cold cases.

Charles Morgan in 1977

One of Tucson's strangest cold cases occurred in 1977, when the body of local escrow agent Charles Morgan was discovered forty miles outside the city limits. The grisly discovery came eleven days after he'd first been reported missing. The thirty-nine-year-old's body was found on the ground near his Mercury Cougar. What makes the cold case an interesting one is that Morgan was found wearing a bulletproof vest and a belt buckle with a concealed knife; he was also armed. It was his weapon, a .357 Magnum, that was used to kill him. He'd been shot execution style in the back of his head.

The media seized on the story, as it was rife with intrigue and questions. What was an escrow agent doing with such a weapon and wearing a bulletproof vest at the time of his murder? What led up to his murder? No fingerprints were found on the weapon, leading to speculation that the killing was a professional hit of some kind. Investigators with the Pima County Sheriff's Department had an interesting case on their hands, one that would remain unsolved.

At the time of Morgan's death, news agencies reported that he worked escrow for alleged crime families and speculated that this may have led to his death. It was also reported that he told people he worked undercover for the Treasury Department. He'd recently testified, in fact, for an investigation on illegal operations at the United States and Mexico border.

The unsolved case was made even odder by the items investigators discovered inside his vehicle. This included one of Morgan's own teeth, found wrapped in a handkerchief. Ammunition, CB radios and several weapons were also found within his car. They also discovered a two-dollar bill fastened to his underwear. On it were written a number of Spanish surnames, as well as a map of the immediate area.

BRIAN LEIGH DAVIS IN 1984

The apartment party on East First Street held on October 19, 1984, had been going on all day. As the day went on, according to nearby residents, it only got louder and more violent. Twenty-four-year-old Brian Davis had gone to the party, as anyone would, to have a good time with friends. He soon found himself confronting another individual who crashed the party at around 8:30 p.m.

Witnesses described the individual Davis confronted as a man with wavy hair and a beard, dressed in dark clothing; he was at least five feet, eight inches tall. The assailant was thought to be between twenty-five and thirty years old. He was seen by at least twenty-five people attending the party.

The confrontation led to a physical altercation between the two inside the confines of the apartment. That fight soon led outside, where the unknown assailant drew a firearm and shot Davis once in the head. The man then fled the scene on a bicycle before police arrived.

Davis was taken to a nearby hospital. He died early the following morning. Investigators were never able to find the bearded man, despite a number of witnesses at the scene, and the investigation has since gone cold.

DEBRA DONOHUE IN 1985

Debra Donohue, a thirty-one-year-old student at the University of Arizona, was found dead in 1985. Her murderer has never been apprehended. *88-Crime.*

Thirty-one-year-old Debra Donohue, a University of Arizona doctoral student, lived in a condominium on Tucson's West Sheryl Drive and worked part time at the Tucson Museum of Art. She would never finish her doctoral work, however.

A friend of hers stopped by for a visit the evening of August 15, 1985, and discovered Donohue's body. When police arrived, they quickly ascertained that she had been killed by strangulation the night before, likely sometime between 11:00 p.m. and 4:00 a.m.

They quickly launched an investigation into the murder and had a suspect in custody. Without sufficient evidence to formally charge the suspect, the Pima County Attorney's Office opted not to prosecute, and the charges were dropped, according to local news reports. Donohue's murder has never been solved.

GALE GREEN IN 1987

At about 6:00 p.m. on October 9, 1987, Gale Green closed her shop, a local lingerie store called Satisfactions, for the evening. She planned to attend a private lingerie show that night, but she wouldn't make it out of her shop alive. Green, forty, had just opened her shop the year before.

When the evening grew late, Green's husband made a call to her brother to report that she hadn't yet arrived home. Her husband said he'd been having car troubles and was unable to check up on her himself. When her brother, David Green, checked on the Country Club Road business, he found the lights on and the door unlocked at 1:30 a.m., which wasn't common for any business. Once inside, he discovered his sister's terrible fate. Sometime between 6:00 p.m. and 7:00 p.m., Gale Green had been brutally attacked and murdered.

According to accounts, she'd been ironing lingerie in preparation for the show when the murder took place. There was a struggle in which Green managed to fend off the attacker with a blow from the iron, which investigators determined would have nicked him, but she was ultimately overpowered. Her killer used the iron to beat her to death, according to news reports. Her brother described the discovery as a "really gruesome scene."

LISA LEANNE ATKINS IN 1988

On April 4, 1988, twenty-two-year-old Lisa LeAnne Atkins was working as a clerk at a local pet store located on West Orange Grove Road. That day, she was working with a male coworker when another man, hooded, entered the store. He approached the two clerks and demanded money from the register. To reinforce his point, he produced a gun and pointed it at the two employees.

Lisa's coworker attempted to use his keys to open the cash register but dropped them. When he bent over to pick them up, the hooded man fired his gun, killing Atkins.

Her murderer was described at the time as a bearded male with sandy brown or dark-blond hair and between twenty-five and forty years of age. He was described as being about five feet, elven inches in height and weighing about 170 pounds. He fled the scene of the shooting in a green, older-model pickup truck with wood siding, according to eyewitnesses.

Just before her death, Atkins had been on the telephone with her mother, who was caring for her son, who was thirteen months old at the time. She had just hung up when the hooded man entered the building. He's not been found.

GAIL PARKER IN 1993

In March 1993, Gail Parker suffered a behavioral breakdown caused by a lack of medication, which she took to control her manic depression. The Tucson-based magazine writer allegedly stopped taking the medication due to the weight gain it caused. Things got so bad that her husband called to have Parker, fifty-one, transported to a local hospital on East Ajo Way. There her psychiatrist was said to meet her for an evaluation—only he never showed up that day. Staff at the hospital declined to admit her, and Parker left the building under her own recognizance, according to family members.

About fifteen hours would pass without a trace of Parker's whereabouts. That changed for the worse, however, when three young bicyclists discovered her body in the desert near East Broadway and South Houghton Road. She was found eleven miles from the hospital; her purse and her jewelry were missing. Investigators determined the cause of death to have been blunt-force trauma to the head. That investigation also revealed that Parker was last seen alive early the morning before, when she entered a convenience store on East Golf Links and South Harrison Road around 1:30 a.m. Later that day, her credit card was used at a gas station in Phoenix.

Parker's family later filed a lawsuit and received a settlement for the incident. One month after her death, her purse also turned up. A fisherman in Kanab, Utah, pulled the item from a lake on U.S. Route 89 north of the Arizona-Utah border. Despite the new development, the case remains cold to this day.

THOMAS STEPHENSON IN 1998

Fifty-eight-year-old retired U.S. Air Force veteran Thomas Stephenson had just finished playing a round of golf at the Davis-Montham Air Base in Tucson and planned to go home and enjoy the rest of his Sunday. That particular day, August 16, 1998, his wife was out of town. But something happened when Stephenson returned home. When he didn't show up for work the following day, his coworkers and family members grew concerned.

Investigators searched the home and found an odd scene. The golf clothes he wore that Sunday at the course were there, as were the remains of a meal. His vehicle, however—a 1985 brown Nissan 300 ZX—was nowhere to be found. A search also revealed a disheveled, slightly askew mattress in the bedroom that was missing a comforter blanket. His glasses, which Stephenson needed in order to drive, were found at the home, leading investigators to believe that Stephenson did not leave alone.

The day after his disappearance, someone used Stephenson's name and credit card to call the Tucson Auto Mall. The caller indicated that the car had broken down and needed a tow for repair. At the time, the vehicle wasn't inspected. It wouldn't be inspected, in fact, until August 22, nearly a week later. It was then that his body was found within the trunk of the vehicle. Stephenson was found strapped down in the hatchback of the Nissan, his body wrapped in the missing comforter and covered with a vehicle sun shade. An autopsy determined that he'd died by asphyxiation.

An investigation into his disappearance also revealed that on the night of his abduction, someone attempted to access his account at a local Tucson ATM. They were believed to be wearing a disguise to avoid recognition by the ATM's camera. Someone also tried to access his account the following day at an ATM in Phoenix. Days following his disappearance, Stephenson's wife also reported a strange and disturbing phone call. Someone on the other end of the line demanded from her a sum of $20,000 and Stephenson's eyeglasses. The caller never said where to deliver the sum, however, and never called back again, leaving his wife helpless to accommodate the request and an investigation without enough evidence to continue.

ANALISSA MONARES-LEON IN 2007

Analissa Monares-Leon was sleeping peacefully in her home on the southwest side of Tucson when she was killed by a bullet. The shot rang out at 5:00 a.m. that October morning, with the bullet passing through the front door of the family's West Dakota Street home located near the intersection of South

Six-year-old Analissa Monares-Leon was sleeping on a couch inside her home when she was struck by a bullet shot from the street outside. Her killer has never been found. *88-Crime.*

Mission and West Irvington Roads. She was sleeping on the couch near the front of the home at the time of the 2007 shooting.

Two men, both thought to be under the age of twenty-five, were seen around the Mission and Irvington Road intersection at the time of the shooting. Both were observed wearing baseball caps. Her murder has never been solved.

LASHAD AMARR "POPE" COOPER IN 2008

Pictured is Lashad Amarr "Pope" Cooper, who was found murdered in the backyard of a vacant property in 2008. Cooper was twenty-two years old. *Homicide Survivors.*

On September 24, 2008, twenty-two-year-old Lashad Cooper joined a friend of his in a parking lot on the southwest side of Tucson. From there, they met up with two more men and made their way to a deserted home on West Ohio Street. It would be the last time Lashad was seen alive.

Cooper's body was soon found in the backyard of the vacant property. Two men were alleged to have fled the scene in a gold-colored Ford Mustang, believed to be a 2000 model. The vehicle is also believed to have had a loud exhaust system, tinted windows and stock wheels. Another two men were also sought in connection to the murder. They're alleged to have fled in a 1990s Honda Civic that also had dark window tinting.

While investigators now think that more people may have been at the scene than originally thought, no new leads have emerged to break open the case.

THE MAN WHO KILLED SANTA

ARIZONA NEWSPAPER EDITOR BLAMED FOR KILLING SANTA CLAUS

John McPhee was a man well known in southern Arizona, particularly in Mesa, Bisbee and nearby Tucson. He worked as managing editor for the *Bisbee Daily Review* in the 1960s before moving to Colorado, where he founded the *Telluride Times* with his wife, Betty. He was even elected mayor of that same town. His name in southern Arizona has not been forgotten.

Unfortunately, it isn't his work in the newspaper industry that made his name so well known throughout the state. McPhee is notorious for his role in the death of none other than Santa Claus. It was a death witnessed by crowds of onlookers, a majority of them children and their parents. Of course, it wasn't the real Saint Nick who perished that winter day in Mesa, thankfully, but a department store dummy dressed in Santa's duds. The children watching didn't know that, though. For them, Santa had died, and it was all McPhee's fault.

The Great Depression, which began with the Wall Street crash in 1929, sparked a wave of despair across the country, leading to widespread homelessness, suicides and hunger. McPhee wanted to help out by spreading a little Christmas cheer. So, with good intentions in his heart, he set out in 1930 to do just that. He and other local merchants wanted to make that year's Christmas parade an exciting one for the children of southern Arizona. McPhee came up with the idea to hire an actor to portray Santa and have him leap from an airplane. He'd pop open a parachute and drop down on the awaiting crowds before leading a parade through town. What could go wrong?

For starters, even actors hired to jump from airplanes were prone to the sadness caused by the Great Depression. For many, alcohol became their only means of comfort. This is what caused this particular Santa Claus to cancel out on McPhee the morning of the big event. He'd simply had too much to drink and therefore could not safely leap into the sky. With time running out, McPhee came up with a backup plan. He made his way to a nearby department store, grabbed a mannequin and dressed it up in a Santa Claus suit. He even got a parachute on its back before getting it loaded onto the plane.

According to McPhee, the idea was to have someone pull the ripcord for the parachute just as the Santa dummy was pushed out of the airplane. It would look like Santa parachuted out, and when the dummy landed, a real Santa Claus waited on the ground to ride in the parade. Only it didn't play out that way.

When the time came to toss the mannequin from the plane, the parachute didn't open as planned, and the Santa Claus stand-in plummeted to the ground—appearing to everyone on the ground as if Santa had perished in the fall. Children were horrified. Parents were incensed. According to many who witnessed the horrific spectacle, screams broke out at the scene of "Santa's dead! Santa's dead!"

From that day forward, McPhee became known as the "Man Who Killed Santa Claus." It was a name destined to follow him the rest of his life, from Mesa to Bisbee and on to Telluride, where he passed away at the age of sixty-six.

An article from the Tucson newspaper the *Arizona Daily Star* quoted McPhee in 1954. "I attempted to rise to the occasion and have the parade with the live Santa but when we arrived it was a ghost town," McPhee said. "From behind closed doors you could hear the wails of heartbroken children. I'm the man who 'killed' Santa Claus and I'm sorry."

GANGSTER JOHN DILLINGER'S VISIT TO THE SOUTHWEST

The Depression of the 1930s may seem like an important marker in the history of America, something to study and hope never occurs again, but for those struggling to survive at the time, the Depression was nothing short of pure hell—beginning with the 1929 stock market crash known to historians as Black Friday, peaking in 1933 and finally coming to a close in 1939. At the Depression's peak, about 15 million Americans were unemployed. Even with half the nation's banks folding, those that remained were often vilified by those who saw all they owned taken away to pay the bills and stay in their home.

Enter John Herbert Dillinger, an American outlaw embraced by many as something akin to a modern-day folk hero. To them, Dillinger took back from those who took everything from the average Joe. For others, he was nothing more than a coldblooded killer whose criminal reign came to an end in Tucson. No matter how it looks, he was one of the most notorious bank robbers in U.S. history. In fact, it's said that he stole more money in one year then Jesse James took in sixteen years. His was a criminal career marked with violence, murder and the chatter of machine gun fire.

He was born on June 22, 1903, in Indiana to John Wilson Dillinger and Mary Ellen "Mollie" Lancaster. When his mother died in 1907, John was only four years old. His older sister, Audrey, raised him at that point, but the young John Dillinger would prove to be a handful for the young woman and her husband. When his father remarried some

American gangster John Dillinger, seen here in this Federal Bureau of Investigations photograph, made his presence known in the Tucson community. *Federal Bureau of Investigations.*

years later, John fell under his guidance once again, although his bad behavior continued. His teen years were marred with petty theft and acts of violence. In 1921, the Dillingers moved to the more rural community of Mooresville, where his father believed young John would be forced to end his criminal tendencies when out of his big-city element. That didn't prove to be the case. He was arrested in 1922 for stealing a vehicle. Despite enlisting in the U.S. Navy the following year, John found himself leaning toward his more rebellious nature once more. Just months after joining, he was dishonorably discharged from service. He served aboard the USS *Utah* but quickly deserted his post when the ship docked in Boston, leaving a seafaring life far behind him.

Although he moved home to Mooresville and married Beryl Ethel Hovious, a life of crime beckoned the young Dillinger. Finding it difficult to keep work, he instead plotted with his friend Ed Singleton to rob the local grocery store. They made off with $50, the modern-day equivalent of about $735. Both were quickly arrested for the crime. Dillinger received a sentence of ten to twenty years for the crime. His term in the Indiana prison system hardened him for his later escapades. It was in prison, according to historical accounts, that he befriended other criminals such as Homer Van Meter and Harry "Pete" Pierpoint, as well as others who shared their knowledge and plotted heists with Dillinger that the group would carry out when released from prison. Beryl and Dillinger divorced in 1929. Later that year, she remarried and moved on with a new life, away from the Dillinger Gang.

Paroled in 1933, Dillinger wasted no time enjoying freedom. He robbed his first bank that same year, making off with $10,000, a considerable haul at the height of the Great Depression. With inflation, that amount would be the equivalent of about $147,000 today. Mere months later, he robbed another Ohio bank but was apprehended and once again thrown in jail.

He wouldn't remain in prison for long. Dillinger's criminal pals, dressed as law enforcement, broke him out of jail, leaving one man, Jess Sarber, dead as a result.

Dillinger and his gang fled to Arizona and holed up in Tucson. Even there, however, the law had a long arm thanks to the sharp eyes of local firefighters. Built in 1919, the Hotel Congress has a long history in downtown Tucson. The Mission/Spanish Revival–style building was constructed in 1918 as part of an expansion of Congress Street.

Registered at the Hotel Congress the night of January 21, 1934, Dillinger and his accomplices settled in with nothing more on their minds than lying low for a spell. At this time, his cohorts consisted of Harry Pierpoint, Charles Makley and Russell Clark. The group had rented a home on North Second Avenue in Tucson, between East Speedway Boulevard and East University Boulevard, but because the floors had been waxed, the decision was made to stay in a hotel. Unfortunately for the gang, a fire would break out in the early morning hours their first night there. The fire, which started in the basement, quickly moved up the floors.

Fire crews were quick to respond and immediately began helping the hotel's occupants out of the building, going so far as to carry luggage and personal belongings for those escaping the fire. With Dillinger's gang, this included bags filled with firearms—a fact that didn't go unnoticed. Firefighters at the scene grew even more suspicious when the gang tipped them $12 for their help (in today's world, that is the equivalent of more than $200). The large sum, combined with the weighty bags, was enough for them to tip off the police.

On January 25, law enforcement moved in. They arrested the members of the gang in various locations throughout Tucson. First to fall into handcuffs was Makley. Police arrested him while he ran an errand. Meanwhile, Clark was apprehended at the rented home on North Second Avenue while Makley, Dillinger and Pierpoint were away. Police convinced Pierpoint to drive to the station on another matter, where he was taken into custody. Dillinger himself was the last member of the gang to be arrested. He was snatched when he returned to the rental house, oblivious to Clark's arrest there earlier in the day. He remarked later that police were smart to arrest the members of his gang, and himself, separately. At the time of his arrest, Dillinger drove a Hudson sedan and was in possession of $9,174 in cash and gold, two submachine guns, five hundred rounds of ammunition, two shortwave police radios and a bulldog puppy. Other guns were also taken during the arrests, as were a handful of bulletproof vests.

WANTED

JOHN HERBERT DILLINGER

On June 23, 1934, HOMER S. CUMMINGS, Attorney General of the United States, under the authority vested in him by an Act of Congress approved June 6, 1934, offered a reward of

$10,000.00

for the capture of John Herbert Dillinger or a reward of

$5,000.00

for information leading to the arrest of John Herbert Dillinger.

DESCRIPTION

Age, 32 years; Height, 5 feet 7-1/8 inches; Weight, 153 pounds; Build, medium; Hair, medium chestnut; Eyes, grey; Complexion, medium; Occupation, machinist; Marks and scars, 1/2 inch scar back left hand, scar middle upper lip, brown mole between eyebrows.

All claims to any of the aforesaid rewards and all questions and disputes that may arise as among claimants to the foregoing rewards shall be passed upon by the Attorney General and his decisions shall be final and conclusive. The right is reserved to divide and allocate portions of any of said rewards as between several claimants. No part of the aforesaid rewards shall be paid to any official or employee of the Department of Justice.

If you are in possession of any information concerning the whereabouts of John Herbert Dillinger, communicate immediately by telephone or telegraph collect to the nearest office of the Division of Investigation, United States Department of Justice,

A 1934 wanted poster for gangster John Dillinger offered a whopping $10,000 for his capture and $5,000 for information on his whereabouts. *Federal Bureau of Investigations.*

Eager to get their man to Indiana, Indiana state police chief Matt Leach himself transported Dillinger back to the Hoosier State. But John Dillinger, already adept at planning escapes, didn't stay inside the walls of the Crown Point jail for long. He soon broke out a second time, using what some believe to be a fake gun he carved, while others claim he used a real gun smuggled in by an accomplice. In either event, Dillinger found himself back on the streets a free man.

His independence was short-lived, however, for on the evening of July 22, 1934, FBI agents zeroed in on the notorious criminal while he took in a movie with two female companions. They moved in to take him when he left Chicago's Biograph Theater, where Dillinger had just finished watching the film *Manhattan Melodrama* starring Clark Gable and Myrna Loy. Three agents descended on Dillinger when he fled into an alley, and all three fired shots when they realized that Dillinger was armed. Bullets struck him four times from behind. He landed face first in the alley, dead from a bullet that entered the back of his neck and exited just under his right eye. He was pronounced dead a short time later at Alexian Brothers Hospital without uttering a single word, according to law enforcement accounts.

His elevated outlaw status brought a throng of onlookers to the alley when he was killed, newspaper reports indicated, and many dipped handkerchiefs and newspapers in his blood to sell as keepsake souvenirs. The Cook County Morgue also made his body available for public viewing, with as many as fifteen thousand visitors coming to see the man over a one-and-a-half-day period. Four death masks were also made following his death—the exit wound from the fatal shot can be seen on them. Collectors have wreaked havoc at Dillinger's grave site at the Crown Hill Cemetery in Indianapolis. His grave marker has been stolen numerous times over the years.

In 2019, efforts were underway to exhume his remains when family members expressed doubts as to whether or not Dillinger had really been killed at the Biograph that fateful night. Working with the History Channel, which planned to televise a story on Dillinger, the family hoped to dig up the body for analysis and cited a number of reasons to do so, including the fact that Dillinger at one time made attempts to burn his fingerprints off. Ultimately, their plans to exhume the corpse failed and, as of January 2020, were canceled.

Today, the Hotel Congress continues to thrive. Following the fire of 1934, the hotel was renovated into a two-story, forty-room property. Over the years, the hotel has become a cultural fixture downtown. In 2003, it

This 1961 photo shows Tucson police sergeant Tom Keeley and secretary Linda Bradfield holding weapons seized from the John Dillinger Gang. Dillinger was captured in Tucson in 1934. *From the* Arizona Daily Star.

was named to the National Register of Historic Places. In 2006 and 2008, the hotel received the Fodor's Choice distinction award. Known as an "urban, historic, rock 'n' roll hotel," Hotel Congress features a number of haunted rooms as well. It's also a mecca for Dillinger aficionados. One weekend each January is dedicated to the capture of John Dillinger. Called Dillinger Days, the annual event features a number of activities, including walking tours, a historical reenactment of Dillinger's capture, a speakeasy and historical artifacts that include an original Tommy gun.

TUCSON'S OTHER GANGSTER

JOE BONANNO AND THE BANANA WARS

The echoes of far-off gunfire can be heard in the streets of Tucson, partially thanks to the city's warm climate, which drew a number of criminal minds to the area.

While John Dillinger was the most famous gangster to hang his hat in the city of Tucson, he wouldn't be the last. Infamous Mafia man Joseph Bonanno also took to the warmer climes of the Southwest in his later years, likely due to his dismissal by many of his fellow Mafiosos. With things getting hot for him in New York, Bonanno made his way to Tucson in 1968 and remained until he died of heart failure at the ripe old age of ninety-two. Bonanno was buried at the Holy Hope Cemetery on North Oracle Road in Tucson. His funeral at Saints Peter and Paul Roman Catholic Church drew about five hundred people, according to media accounts at the time. A good amount of those mourners were believed to have Mafia ties. His crypt carries the inscription "God Family Tradition."

Bonanno, known by the alias Joe Bananas, played a large role in the Mafia's New York operations when he took over his family's business in the 1930s. Those operations are alleged to include prostitution, narcotics, loan sharking and more. He's commonly believed to be one of the influences for the character Michael Corleone in *The Godfather*, written by Mario Puzo and published in 1969, one year after Bonanno relocated to Tucson. While living in Brooklyn, New York, Bonanno worked to develop business ties in Tucson and even sent his children there for school. His son, Bill Bonanno, was a longtime fixture in Tucson. Bill passed away in 2008, six years after his father.

The Banana Wars, also known as the Banana Split, ravaged New York from 1964 to 1969. Bonanno himself, one of the founders of the mob's infamous Five Families, plotted to wrest control of the organization by murdering rival crime bosses. The struggle began in 1964, when his plans to take control were uncovered by the Commission, an American Mafia ruling committee, forcing Bonanno into hiding for eighteen months. He named Bill as his successor before his disappearance. The subsequent mob war led to public shootouts and murders and bled over into Tucson.

The first Tucson-based assault came on July 21, 1968, when the bed of a pickup truck exploded into a debris-ridden fireball. The truck was owned by Pete Licavoli, a Detroit crime boss who also owned a home in Tucson. The following day, bullets riddled Bonanno's Elm Street home in Tucson, and his patio was bombed. A stick of dynamite blew apart a fire pit as well, newspapers reported at the time. Thus the Banana Wars officially opened a new front in Arizona. For a little more than a month in 1968, bombs would explode throughout the city. The coordinated Tucson bombings targeted Bonanno's cohorts and partners who owned businesses in the community. Following the attack at Bonanno's home, a series of two explosions tore into the residence of Peter Notaro, one of Bonanno's allies. According to newspaper accounts, the blast was so massive it was heard twenty blocks away. The Wig Beauty Salon would be the next to come under attack exactly one month later. Located on East Speedway Boulevard, the local business would suffer a second explosion in 1969. In 1968, Joyce Battaglia worked as a receptionist there. She was once married to alleged Mafioso Charles Battaglia and was in the building at the time. Not twenty minutes after the Wig Beauty Salon blast in 1968, a second bomb detonated in the front room of Robert Thomas Smith, a close associate of alleged Tucson mobster Salvatore Spinelli. Particularly remarkable was the newspaper accounts that stated no one was hurt during the explosions. The bombing of Bonanno's home made front-page news the next day in the *Tucson Daily Citizen*.

One law enforcement official, who declined to be named, called the slew of bombings a case of intimidation. "This is obviously a case of retaliation involving Mafia warfare between Bonanno family members and those who oppose him in Tucson. The bombings were done for intimidation, as a way of saying they can go further."

By November of that year, Bonanno had stepped down, giving up control of his crime family, and moved to Tucson permanently. He'd fall into hot water with the Mafia again, however, when he published his autobiography, *A Man of Honor*, in 1983. Sharing his story is alleged to have broken the

Mafioso Joseph Bonanno moved to Tucson in 1968 and passed away on May 11, 2002. His grave can be seen at the Holy Hope Cemetery on Oracle Road. *Author's collection.*

Mafia's Code of Silence, known as the Omertà. He lived under fear of death from that day forward, although no hit was ever carried out successfully.

Coincidentally, Federal Bureau of Investigations (FBI) agent William F. Roemer Jr., famous for his battles against organized crime, also retired to the Tucson community and lived near Bonanno. During his thirty-year career, Roemer dealt with a number of organized crime figures, and after his retirement, he even wrote biographies of some of the more notable gangsters he'd encountered. This includes his books *Enforcer: Spilotro: The Chicago Mob's Man Over Las Vegas*, *War of the Godfathers* and *Accardo: The Genuine Godfather*. He traveled the country to share his experiences and often appeared on television shows as a guest. Over his decorated career, Roemer tackled such famous mobsters as Samuel "Mooney" Giancana, Felix Anthony "Milwaukee Phil" Alderisio, Samuel "Mad Sam" DeStefano and, of course, Bonanno. He, in fact, had his own nickname, which he earned during his years at the University of Notre Dame. While studying for a legal degree, he showed proficiency at the sport of boxing, which earned him the moniker "Zip" Roemer.

Roemer joined the FBI in 1950 and became the Bureau's most highly decorated agent during the course of his career. He retired in 1980 after moving to Tucson in 1978 to be near one of his children. Besides his work against mobsters, he was also known for his part in the investigation around missing Teamster leader Jimmy Hoffa. Roemer died from lung cancer in 1996 at the age of sixty-nine. He passed away two days before he would have turned seventy. Roemer was a member of the Tucson Chapter of the Society of Former Special Agents of the FBI.

THE UNIVERSITY OF ARIZONA'S FIRST FEMALE PROFESSOR

LOUISE FOUCAR MARSHALL'S DARK STORY

The university boom made a large impact on the Tucson community in 1885 after the federal government granted land to every state, and territories, for the sole purpose of creating institutes of higher learning. The goal was to make college education more attainable to Americans across the country. Territorial legislature made the University of Arizona the first in the state that year. Enrollment for the first wave of students began in 1891. About twenty years later, the university offered three colleges: letters, arts and sciences consisted of one, while the College of Mines and Engineering and the College of Agriculture made up the others. Others followed, particularly after World War II, when the university opened colleges in multiple health-related fields.

Today, the University of Arizona covers more than 380 acres across downtown Tucson. Featuring a number of museums open to the public, from anthropology to art, the university is considered by many to be a miniature "city within a city." Nicknamed "Science City," the university is also well known academically for its many programs and its connections to the National Aeronautics and Space Administration (NASA) due to the observatory located on the campus.

One of the university's most well-known characters, Louise Foucar Marshall, will forever be remembered as the institution's first female professor. She's also remembered for a darker tale involving infidelity and the sharp report of gunfire. Later, she would become known for her philanthropic lifestyle and the subsequent creation of the Marshall Foundation in Tucson.

Louise Foucar Marshall, seen here in this 1901 photograph, became the first female professor at the University of Arizona in 1900. *Marshall Foundation.*

Louise Henriette Foucar was born in Boston in 1864 to a German immigrant family. Her father is credited with discovering patent leather, which provided a sizable income for the family. This allowed Louise to travel the world for study. She traveled to Italy, France, Switzerland, Texas and Mexico. After a brief stint in Denver, Colorado, where she earned two degrees, Louise continued on to Arizona in 1898. With heart issues and tuberculosis, she strived to find a climate conducive to her health. Living during the Victorian era taught young Louise the restraint and formal behavior attributed to that era—at least in most respects. She began her graduate studies in Tucson but was quickly recommended for a staff position there.

By 1900, Louise had been named the first female professor at the university, where she taught botany. She was thirty-six. Louise also taught English, French, Latin and Spanish. One year later, she was made head of the department for ancient and modern languages. In this period, the university was home to about 20 staff members, who looked over about 150 students. Around this time, she also began to buy up land around the university using family funds.

Louise met Thomas Marshall in 1903 when she hired him to help maintain her properties. Marshall, a former student from the university, married Louise in 1904. The two were married in Texas due to Louise's aversion to publicity. The couple lived together on a two-acre lot in Louise's brick home off East Second Street. By 1922, Louise was a well-known figure in the Tucson community. She developed businesses along what is today known as University Boulevard, including the Park Avenue Shops, Tucson's first suburban shopping center. By 1930, she'd begun the Marshall Charitable Foundation, today known more simply as the Marshall Foundation. From a young age, Louise hoped to make a difference in the lives of those less fortunate than her.

Around this time, Louise began to get sick. Rumors circulated that her husband was in the midst of an affair, allegedly with a former housekeeper. As her illness continued, Louise went to see a number of doctors to determine the cause of her condition. She underwent weeks of testing and learned that she was the victim of poisoning. According to reports, it was suspected that arsenic had been periodically introduced into her body. She suspected Thomas and the ex-housekeeper of being behind the slow poisoning, and on the night of April 27, 1931, she shot him in a fit of rage five times at point-blank range. Three of the five bullets fired that night hit him in nonvital organs. The other two bullets missed him completely.

Thomas was taken to Los Angeles to undergo treatment for the gunshot wounds. He died three weeks later, but not from the bullets—though certainly from resulting complications. According to most reports, Thomas died from an infection that resulted from a poorly performed operation. Louise, however, was promptly charged with first-degree murder. Due to her prominence in the community, the incident became a media sensation in Tucson and was covered extensively in local newspapers. Louise found herself under severe scrutiny, despite her protests that she had only intended to warn her husband off.

The media attention forced Louise's lawyers, Tucson attorneys James Boyle and George Darnell, to successfully petition that the trial be moved to Nogales. They used for their defense temporary insanity. She pleaded

Pictured is Geronimo Plaza, home of the Marshall Foundation, which Louise Foucar Marshall founded in the 1930s as the Marshall Charitable Foundation. *Author's collection.*

guilty under those circumstances. In fact, many claim that the case counted as one of the first to use the defense successfully. After what was reportedly a highly emotional case, in which Louise testified to her fears of being poisoned and how it led her to commit the shooting, she was acquitted of the first-degree murder charge. The jury deliberated for only half an hour before making its decision.

With that dark chapter behind her, Louise refocused on her nonprofit work and real estate business. Soon she became the manager for the organization's daily operations, working with a newly created board of directors. According to the Marshall Foundation, Louise died at the age of ninety-two in 1956 with only $5,000 in her bank account. The foundation, however, was worth an estimated $900,000. In 2014 alone, the foundation collected money from seventy-six commercial and retail tenants and donated more than $1 million to Tucson charities and scholarships. The organization owns most of the property at the Main Gate Square retail area, located between Park and Euclid Avenues on University Boulevard. By 2015, the foundation had given in total $11.3 million in scholarships to the University of Arizona.

PIED PIPER OF TUCSON

SERIAL MURDERER CHARLES SCHMID

The 1960s were a different time, full of cultural shifts and a change in the fabric of America, from civil rights reform to scientific breakthroughs. Roald Dahl published his book *Charlie and the Chocolate Factory*, and the Beatles soared to number one on the charts in 1964. Muhammad Ali became the heavyweight world champion, and the first Ford Mustang rolled off the assembly line.

In Arizona, Senator Barry Goldwater announced his intention to land the Republican nomination for president of the United States. While he did indeed land the nomination, Goldwater ultimately lost the election to Lyndon B. Johnson in a landslide defeat. He is credited, however, with the creation of the conservative movement that is still prevalent among many Republicans to this day.

It was in this climate of social change and Arizona conservatism that young Charles "Smitty" Schmid Jr. rose to infamy as the murderous "Pied Piper of Tucson," as he was named by journalist Don Moser of *Life* magazine. In 1964, Schmid stood at five feet, three inches in height. He'd hang out on Speedway Boulevard dressed in his jeans with the cuffs rolled up and wearing face makeup he believed added to his tough charisma. That charisma and threatening demeanor worked, too, as the silence that surrounded the murders would prove. He reportedly also dyed the hairs on his arms and chest and worked hard to make his eyebrows just right each day.

Time magazine wrote of Schmid that he "always had wheels, money, tall tales and an inexhaustible supply of available girls' phone numbers."

Charles Schmid was born in 1942 and died in 1975. Pictured here during his 1966 trial, Schmid was nicknamed the "Pied Piper of Tucson." *From the* Arizona Daily Star.

Born in 1942, Schmid was the adopted son of Tucson nursing home owners Charles and Katherine Schmid. Young Smitty didn't get along well with his adopted father in those early years. Katherine would later seek a divorce, according to historical records. Seeking to connect with his birth parents, Charles Jr. met with his real mother at one point but was quickly told never to return. Generally considered attractive and intelligent, Schmid traded on his looks and charm more than intellect. Often he'd tell tall tales—that he'd been put in a stretching machine at birth due to a stunted birth or that he'd had leukemia—and he also shared with his unscrupulous friends that he knew every con in the book. Many of those cons he'd use on his family members in order to get money, although he'd tell his friends the money came from nefarious Mexican sources or women who paid him to teach them love-making techniques.

He suffered poor grades throughout school. It's often said that he compensated for his short stature by stuffing whatever he could find into his boots, often cowboy boots, to make himself appear taller. He would dye his hair black and, as a finishing touch, apply an odd mixture of makeup to his face along with a smear of white lipstick to make his mouth look pale. On his skin, he'd apply tan-colored pancake makeup and a faux beauty mark on his cheek he made from axle grease and a small bit of putty.

Following high school, it's believed that Schmid lived off his parents' income. He never made an effort to find employment on his own. Despite all of this, Schmid was something of a ladies' man, a fact he often boasted about in an odd way. "I can manifest my neurotical emotions, emancipate an epicureal instinct, and elaborate on my heterosexual tendencies," he would say, according to some news reports.

When the spring of 1964 rolled around, Schmid dated a teen named Mary French, described by some as a frumpy seventeen-year-old. By late May, he had confided in her, as well as his comrade John Saunders, that he wanted to kill someone—a girl in particular.

It was French, according to all accounts, who lured a young fifteen-year-old from her home not long after their deadly discussion. Alleen Rowe had been promised a party, and when her mother left for the evening to her job as a night nurse, she snuck out to meet French. There would be no party. Instead, Schmid, French and Saunders took the girl to the desert outskirts of Tucson. She was raped by the two men, who later bludgeoned her with a stone. While they buried her, French buried the hair curlers the girl had been wearing at the time, according to historical accounts.

During a subsequent police investigation into the young teen's disappearance, both French and Schmid were questioned by the authorities and admitted that they planned to take her to a party but said she was nowhere to be found when they arrived to pick her up. With both stating the same thing, police moved their investigation elsewhere. A bulletin dispatched by Tucson police at the time described Rowe as wearing a one-piece black bathing suit, a blouse covered in yellow flowers and orange flipflops.

Soon, Schmid's ego would get the best of him. With a new friend, ex–reform school troublemaker Richie Bruns, it wasn't long before Schmid was boasting to him about the killing. His friend Saunders, by this time, had joined the U.S. Navy and moved on with his life. Schmid was also seeing a new girl, sixteen-year-old Gretchen Fritz, whom he'd also told about the murder. Fritz was also considered a troublemaker in school, despite being the daughter of a notable local heart doctor. Her partying, drinking and dominant lifestyle may have been part of what drove her to date Schmid. Rowe's killer, meanwhile, worried that he had told one too many people about the murder, particularly when things got rocky with Fritz due to what Bruns described as her controlling nature. By August, things weren't looking good between the two, and on August 16, 1965, their relationship came to a brutal end.

Fritz and her little sister, Wendy, thirteen, were on their way to see Elvis Presley in his latest film. They told their parents where they were going and left for the movies. The sisters were never seen again. With Rowe's disappearance preceding them, the community of Tucson grew uneasy. Locals as well as police began to search for the missing girls, following every lead. Even Joe Bonanno involved himself in the search, with the local Mafioso interviewing both Schmid and Bruns, according to the latter. Schmid feigned ignorance as to their whereabouts throughout.

However, just as he had the year before, Schmid struck again. The two girls were buried in the desert, with the help of Bruns, whom he convinced to help him. But Bruns wasn't the same man he'd been before. The weight of the secret began to weigh on him, especially when he fell for a young woman some months later. According to accounts, Bruns worried that

Schmid would come after his new love interest out of fear that she might go to authorities and turn him in. In fact, Bruns contended that she was under surveillance and that he'd once caught Schmid driving by her house in the middle of the night, with the headlights turned off, after his girl reported that she'd seen someone hanging around outside of her bedroom window. According to Bruns, his new girlfriend had once been engaged to Schmid, but the relationship ended when she wouldn't commit to sharing a bank account with him. After that, Bruns began to date her.

In October 1965, when the United States began bombing raids in Cambodia and left-handed pitcher Sandy Koufax and the Los Angeles Dodgers took home the pennant over the Milwaukee Braves, Bruns paid a visit to Tucson police. He told them everything he knew and took them to the unmarked desert graves of the two Fritz girls.

Bruns would go on to write the book *I, a Squealer: The Insider's Account of the Pied Piper of Tucson Murders*, detailing his time with Schmid. In it, Bruns talked about Schmid's physical strength, wrapped in a small body, and shared conversations that he'd had with the man about the murders. It's often believed that Schmid may have continued his murderous rampage had Bruns not blown the whistle.

Following the grisly discovery, police wasted no time hauling in those involved in the first killing, arresting Schmid, his former girl French and Saunders. The latter both admitted to the murder and agreed to testify against Schmid. Saunders, nonetheless, was later sentenced to life in prison. He was nineteen at the time of his sentencing. French, also nineteen at the time, got off with a scant five years for her involvement in the murder. Others were also believed to have known about the murders. Some speculated that at least thirty individuals in Tucson may have been aware of Schmid's dark secret, although Bruns was the only one who stepped forward.

The next year, Schmid faced trial for the murders and was quickly found guilty and eligible for the death penalty. The hiccup was that Rowe's body had not yet been located. While French and Saunders told police where it was located, and her buried curlers were found, the body was no longer where they had buried it. This led to a murder plea without a death sentence. Schmid, then twenty-three, was later sentenced to fifty years to life behind bars. He eventually hoped for a retrial, however, and told investigators where the body could be found. The killer had reburied her body without telling anyone. He hoped to show that Rowe had not died from a blow to the head as Saunders claimed, yet an autopsy showed that she had, in fact, died from just such a wound. A retrial was subsequently denied.

Nearly ten years after his trial, and following numerous unsuccessful prison escapes, Schmid himself was murdered by two other inmates, ending his sentence early. The attack occurred on March 20, 1975. According to reports, he was stabbed more than twenty times, including in the eye, in the lungs and across his abdomen. Despite efforts by medical staff, he succumbed to his injuries ten days later on March 30. His gravestone can be found at the Florence State Prison Cemetery.

A year before, he had legally changed his name to Paul David Ashley, believing that a new name would help his rehabilitation.

The Pied Piper case is thought to have been the inspiration behind the Joyce Carol Oates story "Where Are You Going, Where Have You Been?" The story was later adapted into the film *Smooth Talk*, starring Laura Dern.

THE STORY OF LEWIS SIROTTA

GANGLAND HIT?

Mickey's Restaurant off Speedway Boulevard in Tucson offered daily specials for fifty cents in the early 1960s, which included an entrée, garlic bread, a potato and a veggie. Things were different then when it came to the cost of a meal. Mickey's is no longer in business and the area where it was located is now a CVS Pharmacy, but the story of Lewis Sirotta is very much alive and well.

At quarter to midnight on January 2, 1960, Lewis Sirotta left for Mickey's from his home in midtown Tucson after getting numerous telephone calls at his home. According to accounts of the night, the forty-nine-year-old intended to meet someone for a late-night business deal. A waitress at the restaurant, however, told authorities that he never met anyone inside the place. When he left, two additional figures were observed in the back seat of his Oldsmobile sedan. No one thought much about it until the next day, when a construction worker, Nazario Abasta, saw the sedan parked near the intersection of Silverbell and Sunset Road and reported it. Pima County Sheriff's Department deputies towed the vehicle to a body shop. Upon further investigation, they discovered Sirotta's body in the trunk of his car. He'd been strangled by a wire or cord, a method known as "garroting," and a later autopsy revealed that he'd also ingested a knockout drug. He'd been dead about twenty-four hours before his body was discovered, according to the same autopsy.

Pictured is Lewis Sirotta, who was found murdered in January, 1960. His killers have never been apprehended, although many speculated that the murder was a gangland-style hit. *From the* Arizona Daily Star.

Many speculated at the time that the murder was a gangland hit, although the crime itself has never been solved. Sirotta was a promoter and land developer who moved to Tucson from North Hollywood, California, five years before his death. He'd suffered bad business deals leading up to his murder. Also, according to newspapers, he was connected to a number of criminal characters. Sirotta himself, however, had no criminal record. At the time of his death, he worked as a project manager for the Coronet Park Development Company on East Drexel Road. He was also associated with the Tanque Verde Park Central organization, which had planned a $9.5 million development in the city.

Two years prior to his death, Sirotta was also involved with another man in a mining operation in California's Santa Cruz County. His associate, Anthony Doria, was under investigation by federal authorities for his role as a Teamsters union official.

Newspapers would speculate as to the motive for the death and publicly warned criminals from bringing gangland-style tactics to Tucson.

TUCSON'S HISTORY OF VIOLENCE

THE 1967 RIOTS

Racial tensions were at an all-time high in 1967. Riots erupted across the nation that year in more than one hundred cities coast to coast. According to estimates published in the *U.S. News & World Report*, about 177 individuals were thought to have been killed as a result of rioting, with thousands more suffering injuries. Property damage was estimated to cost more than $1 billion.

While there wasn't a single cause for the incidents, according to media at the time, racial relations were strained during that period due to a number of factors. Racial inequality was likely a large part of it. Violent encounters with law enforcement, and prejudice, were widely reported. In that period, strides were made in some areas to combat the incidents and make forward progress in equal rights. Congress passed the Civil Rights Act, and the Supreme Court lifted a ban on interracial marriage, among other achievements. Proposed by President John F. Kennedy, the Civil Rights Act passed in 1964 and eliminated segregation in public places. The act also banned job discrimination based on race, color, religion, sex or cultural origin.

Kennedy said at the time that the United States "will not be fully free until all of its citizens are free." President Lyndon B. Johnson immediately took up the fight for equal rights after Kennedy was assassinated in November 1963.

While widespread rioting occurred across the country, including Milwaukee, New Jersey and Los Angeles, the riots in Detroit, Michigan, are largely considered the most violent. Between July 23 and July 28, 1967, forty-three people died and about two thousand were injured. Property damage estimates in Detroit were somewhere between $250 and $500 million. This resulted from the thousands of stores that were looted during this period, about 1,700 according to media reports, combined with about 1,400 fires that were also started during the rioting. The U.S. Army and the National Guard were brought in to help local law enforcement. Over that one-week period, more than seven thousand arrests were made, according to newspaper accounts from the time. Considered to be one of the largest civil disturbances in American history, the riots are commonly known today as the Detroit Rebellion of 1967.

Tucson was not immune to civil unrest during that year. Clashes with police occurred during the same period as the events in Detroit, with further rioting breaking out north in Phoenix. The Tucson Riots of 1967 came on the heels of the arrest of a fourteen-year-old Black teen. More than two hundred people gathered to protest Tucson police between Fourth Avenue and Seneca Street.

At the time, the *Los Angeles Times* reported on the Tucson Riots, citing "minor violence." When compared to Detroit and other cities, Tucsonans were indeed lucky that the violence didn't escalate. Reports at the time indicate that a liquor store was targeted by sixty rioters and suffered the most damage. Injuries were also reported from the riots, but none was said to be life-threatening. Tucson police, firefighters and members of the National Guard were called to the scene of the liquor store. Rocks were thrown at civilians, police vehicles and buildings during the riots. A fire bomb was also reportedly thrown at a paint store, causing minimal damage. The day the Tucson Riots ended, they began two hours north in Phoenix.

Tucsonans took immediate action to remedy the unrest. Many meetings were held between community leaders and elected city officials. The groups hoped to avoid future conflicts by discussing and understanding the events that caused the rioting and what could be done to avoid such acts in the future. The meeting included members of the NAACP, the local chairman of the Congress of Racial Inequality and members of Tucson City Council. On July 28 of that year, just days after the riot, a second meeting offered residents of Tucson's south side the chance to speak publicly about their issues with local law enforcement, the lack of youth resources and local unemployment matters.

President John F. Kennedy speaks to the people of the United States on the topic of civil rights. He addressed the nation from the Resolute Desk in this photograph from June 1963. *National Park Service.*

This led to a number of positive changes in the Tucson community. City staff agreed to leave a local youth center, Mirasol, open late into the night to give local youth a place to hang out other than the streets. The incidents also led to the creation of the Job Project, a program designed to give temporary jobs to the "chronically unemployed." Temp jobs were subsequently found for sixty individuals, with the promise of possible full-time employment also offered. More than four hundred jobs were eventually offered to members of the African American community as a result, according to news reports at the time.

PIONEER HOTEL FIRE

TRAGEDY AND PANIC, TWENTY-NINE KILLED

One of Tucson's worst tragedies befell the community just days before Christmas on December 20, 1970.

Twenty-nine people perished in a fire at the Pioneer Hotel. Among those who died were Harold and Margaret Steinfeld, the owners of the Steinfeld Department Store. The husband and wife lived on the ninth floor of the hotel. Built in 1929 by Albert Steinfeld, the large, eleven-story downtown building was said at the time to be "absolutely fireproof." He bought the property where the hotel would be built in 1909. Prior to the hotel, the corner of Stone and Pennington Avenue was the home of a Methodist church. By 1910, the site was serving as railroad offices for the Southern Pacific of Mexico and the Epes Randolph Lines. Steinfeld did not own the hotel by the time the fire occurred. He sold his interests in the building to other Tucson business leaders in 1963. By 1977, the building would undergo extensive remodeling work. More upgrades would also be added to the interior sections years later.

The building is currently used as business offices. To this day, a definitive cause for the fire has yet to be determined.

Reports of flames first circulated among hotel residents shortly after midnight that fateful December night. Fire crews hurried ladders to the scene of the blaze, but more than an hour later, as the flames spread and the heat intensified, they found themselves unable to reach everyone in time. Some waited on balconies, according to reports, but vanished by

Twenty-nine people died in the 1970 fire at the Pioneer Hotel in downtown Tucson. The fire occurred during a Christmas party for a local aircraft company. *From the* Arizona Daily Star.

the time help arrived. Others created makeshift ropes out of sheets and other material to lower themselves to safety as the interior staircases were reported to be swallowed in fire. Others were not able to reach safety in time, according to an initial report in the December 20, 1970 edition of the *Arizona Daily Star*.

The newspaper reported one witness at the time of the blaze as saying, "People were jumping from the windows and splattering on the sidewalk. It was awful. Firemen were screaming to people through their horns to stay on the floors for oxygen." Firefighters attempted to communicate with those on the higher floors, shouting at them to resist jumping from the building. That command was reportedly issued in Spanish and English, according to reports.

Initial reports indicated that people were jumping from the tenth floor and from the rooftop to escape the flames. While the first newspaper account indicated only two confirmed deaths as a result of the blaze, it was clear that this number would increase dramatically.

Ladders were used on Stone and Pennington Avenue to reach the fire victims. Some were rescued as they waited on window ledges. Many of the building's fire escapes were inaccessible due to the fire's terrible hunger, making an easy escape from the conflagration impossible.

Besides local firefighters, officers with the Tucson Police Department, the Sheriff's Department, U.S. Border Patrol and more responded to the scene to offer what assistance they could. Newspaper accounts also identified Father Calehare, with St. Augustine's Cathedral, as he performed last rites to a fire victim on the second floor. The lower floors of the hotel, up to the third level, were accessible, although many were unable to climb further due to fire and smoke. One firefighter, Arth Apodaca, fell four floors as he attempted rescues of those trapped in the hotel. Luckily, it was reported that he sustained noncritical injuries as a result of the fall.

While the Pioneer Hotel would normally qualify for inclusion in the National Register of Historic Places, damage from the fire, and subsequent remodeling, prevented this. It's historic nonetheless for its more dire history. The Pioneer Hotel Fire is still considered the deadliest in Arizona history.

A sixteen-year-old teen named Louis C. Taylor was subsequently arrested for starting the fire. He was sentenced to life in prison on multiple counts of murder. That sentence was a controversial one, however, as the evidence used against him was considered by many to be inadequate for a conviction. The Arizona Justice Project, made up of law students and attorneys, worked to overturn that conviction, and in 2013, Taylor

The Pioneer Hotel building as it looks today. When it was constructed in 1929, the structure was considered the area's first "skyscraper." *Author's collection.*

was finally released. Taylor, a biracial teen, was originally tried by an all-white jury, leading many to wonder whether a racial bias influenced their decision due to racial tension in Tucson at the time.

Taylor said that he went to the hotel that fateful night to drink. A local business, using the venue for a holiday party that night, made a great target for free alcohol. When the fire broke out, he joined in the rescue effort by knocking on doors and helping to load victims on stretchers, according to accounts.

By the time of his release in 2013, forty-two years later, Taylor had spent a majority of his life behind bars. He struggled to adapt to his new life, according to media interviews following his release. Taylor never faltered in declaring his innocence in connection to the 1970 fire. He was arrested in 2017 for armed robbery. At the time, the sixty-three-year-old was accused of assaulting a clerk at an inn with a baseball bat before leaving the business with an undisclosed amount of money. He was later captured by Tucson police after they reviewed security footage and collected forensic evidence at the scene.

TUCSON'S STORM OF THE CENTURY

HOW TUCSON BRAVED THE OCTAVE ONSLAUGHT

When most people think of Arizona, they see in their minds vast stretches of dusty land, tall cacti holding out their arms, coyotes braying at the moon and rolling tumbleweeds. Some think of cattle and cowboys, gunfights and weather-worn barns. What they don't often think of is rain. But Arizona does get occasional rainstorms, heavy monsoons that wreak havoc in the summer and brutal snowstorms in northern Arizona. At times, the rainfall can become so heavy, in fact, that homes are destroyed and people lose their lives in flash floods. In 1983, the destruction and loss of life came from Tropical Storm Octave. The storm is still considered one of Arizona's worst tropical cyclones in the state's history.

The disturbance began on September 23, 1983, off the Gulf of Tehuantepec. When the storm moved into Arizona, it brought with it an onslaught of water. In Tucson, rivers were reported to reach eight feet deep. A number of rivers in southern Arizona—such as the Santa Cruz, Rillito and Gila Rivers—recorded their highest crests ever. A number of towns, including Marana outside of the Tucson city limits, were completely flooded. Residents whose homes were submerged in the torrential floods had to be quickly evacuated. In nearby Clifton, about seven hundred homes were completely destroyed by Octave. In all it's estimated that three thousand buildings were destroyed by the raging storm. About 10,000 people in total were left homeless following the storm. Overall, damage in the state was estimated at about $500 million. Pima County was declared by President Ronald Reagan to be a "major disaster area." Other counties to receive

Tropical Storm Octave tore through the state of Arizona, including many parts of Tucson, as seen in this photograph from 1983. Fourteen people were reported drowned as a result of the storm. *From the* Arizona Daily Star.

that designation included Pinal, Santa Cruz, Yavapai, Cochise, Gila and Graham. About $650,000 in aid was distributed to those who lost everything as a result of the storm. Fifteen shelters were created for victims as well, in all holding 2,905 people.

Fourteen people were reported drowned as a result of the tropical storm. Almost one thousand people were injured.

The heavy rains lasted in southern Arizona from September 28 to October 4. Floodwaters in Tucson reached at least eight feet deep, according to some reports. Many residents were stranded on the rooftops of homes to escape the rushing water. Most of Tucson, in fact, experienced flooding of some kind. According to media reports, only two residents in nearby Marana owned flood insurance. One flood official, according to news accounts, said that they had been told by city officials that flooding simply couldn't occur there. Described as Tucson's "Storm of the Century," Octave caused between $54 and $100 million in damages in the city. Infrastructure such as roads and bridges were destroyed or severely compromised in some cases. The storm is still considered one of the worst in the history of Pima County.

Octave became the perfect storm. That year, Arizona's monsoon storms arrived later than usual, drenching the southern landscape with far more rain than is typical for that time of year. With a wet winter prior to their arrival, the ground was already quite saturated by the time Octave rolled into town. Noting the unusual weather patterns, the National Weather Service issued warnings to residents in conjunction with the Phoenix National Weather Service.

Floods are not uncommon in Tucson's history, as there have been others both before and after the great flood of 1983. On September 10, 1887, flooding devastated portions of the city, according to newspaper accounts. Railroad tracks and washed-out rivers were reported in the *Arizona Daily Star* at the time, with some stating that floodwaters were more than nine feet deep. More flooding occurred in 1914, according to newspaper accounts. On December 23, days before Christmas, raging waters tore through southern Arizona once again, killing several people and leaving at least twenty-five individuals stranded on rooftops. More flooding occurred years later in 1965. On December 21 and December 31 of that year, the *Arizona Daily Star* followed another large flood in the Tucson area. Rillito Creek, north of downtown Tucson, overflowed due to inclement weather on December 21, washing out a trailer park in the Flowing Wells neighborhood. Two trailers were reported destroyed. Those fears resurfaced just over a week later when the creek bulged due to melting snow from the Catalina Mountains and heavy rain.

Another flood would arrive a decade later when heavy rains from the Pacific Ocean marched across Arizona. From January 6 to January 19, 1993, a series of storms battered the state, causing widespread flooding. In Tucson, Tanque Verde Creek was one of the first to overflow. The floods of 1993 caused an estimated $12 million in damages in Pima County alone. Subsequent years have seen further flooding throughout the southern parts of Arizona. These include floods of 2005, 2006, 2008, 2010 and beyond.

Tucson's monsoon season typically begins in June of each year and ends in September, although the rains have occasionally started late and lasted longer. Monsoon season is commonly associated with thunderstorms, high levels of humidity, flash flooding, hailstorms, high winds and extreme heat prior to the storm's arrival. Flash flooding is an annual concern in most of Arizona due to the heavy amounts of rainfall associated with the storms. According to the National Weather Service, flooding that occurs within six (but typically three) hours of rainfall events can be considered a flash flood. The floods can occur due to mudslides or levee or dam breaks. What can be a small creek or stream can become an angry body of water following a flash flood. And often, these floods can be deadly.

Flash flooding has long been a concern in the Tucson community. This includes a 1945 incident in which ten people died when the bridge they were on in Benson washed out due to a flash flood. Four vehicles in total were washed off the bridge into Julian wash, located just southwest of Tucson. Eight people were reported drowned in a flash flood at Tanque Verde Falls on July 26, 1981, including one eleven-year-old child. In 2017, a raging flash flood killed ten members of a family on the Tonto National Forest at a popular swimming spot. The family members were there to celebrate a birthday when the flood hit.

THE NATION'S FIRST STALKING LAWS

THE TUCSON CONNECTION

From a young age, Rebecca Schaeffer was on track for stardom. After becoming a teen model, the young woman made her way to New York City when she was old enough, with a mind to become more than just a pretty face. She hoped to make it big in show business. Soon she landed a role on the daytime soap opera *One Life to Live*. Her big break would come in 1986, however, when she was offered a starring role opposite Pam Dawber on the sitcom *My Sister Sam*. The show ran for forty-four episodes between 1986 and 1988. Schaeffer even appeared on the cover for the March 1987 issue of *Seventeen* magazine.

After appearing in several movies, her star continued to rise in the public eye. This included a role in the film *Godfather III*, which had yet to start filming. It was during this period that the twenty-one-year-old lost her life to a man who had been following her movements for months, a man whose crimes would lead to the beginning of the current stalker laws in the United States. Her killer, nineteen-year-old Robert John Bardo, was eventually charged with her death.

Bardo confronted Schaeffer at the door to her West Hollywood home on July 18, 1989, after finding her address with the help of a private investigator and motor vehicle records. According to media outlets, he was unhappy that the actress, who played a more wholesome character on television, had performed a sex scene in one of her movies. He'd been following the actress for years, according to accounts, and a particular scene in the film *Scenes from the Class Struggle in Beverly Hills* didn't sit well with him.

Bardo allegedly tried to gain entry to the set of *My Sister Sam* years before as well, although at that time he was turned away by security. After confronting Schaeffer, Bardo appeared to leave, although he wouldn't stay away for long.

Publicity still of Rebecca Schaeffer for the 1980s sitcom *My Sister Sam*, which launched Schaeffer's career. She was murdered by a fan in 1989. *CBS Network.*

He returned about an hour later, this time with a .357 magnum, and shot the young actress point blank in the chest. According to psychologists, Bardo felt as though the actress had personally betrayed him by appearing in the sex scene. Although he later told law enforcement that he considered suicide after he shot Schaeffer, he did nothing of the kind that day. When he fled the scene, Bardo allegedly tossed a book he carried on his person into nearby bushes. The book, J.D. Salinger's *Catcher in the Rye*, is also the book John Lennon's murderer carried on his person when he committed his foul act. Since then, Bardo has claimed that it was a mere coincidence that he had the same book as the infamous Mark David Chapman at the time.

Bardo did, however, cite another gruesome incident as his inspiration for the attack. *People* magazine in 1982 published an article on the attempted murder of actress Theresa Saldana, who was featured in the film *Raging Bull*. She survived an attack by Arthur Jackson at her home. She died in 2016 due to complications with pneumonia. Jackson was sentenced to twelve years for the attack. It was the article in *People* magazine, Bardo said, that gave him the idea to murder Schaeffer.

Bardo grew up in the Tucson community. He attended Chaparral Junior High School in the Sunnyside Unified School District. Later, he worked as a custodian at a fast-food restaurant before making his way to Los Angeles. Following the heinous murder, Bardo fled to Tucson but was soon arrested. The day after killing Schaeffer, he was found running in traffic on Interstate 10 near West Congress Street.

Bardo was sentenced to life in prison for the murder, but his incarceration didn't keep him out of the limelight. In 2007, Bardo himself was attacked by another inmate at Mule Creek State Prison in Amador County. According to media reports, he was stabbed a total of eleven times. Bardo was stabbed in the prison yard as many of the inmates were being sent to breakfast. Two homemade weapons were found at the scene of the attack. It was not known whether his notorious murder was a motive behind the attack. Bardo was treated for his injuries and sent back to prison to recover. He was housed in a maximum-security unit for inmates with special needs. According to newspaper accounts, the inmates included those convicted of sex crimes, former gang members and notorious criminals. His attacker was identified as a man serving an eighty-plus-year sentence for second-degree murder.

Despite attempts to argue that Bardo suffered from mental illness, Deputy District Attorney Marsha Clark made a case for obsession, and in 1991, he was found guilty of first-degree murder and sentenced to life behind bars. There would be no possibility for parole. A year before his sentencing, the State of California took steps to safeguard those victimized by stalkers. The state passed its first anti-stalking laws in 1990, one year after Rebecca's murder, making it harder to obtain personal information through the motor vehicles department. The law "makes it a felony to cause another, or their family, to be in reasonable fear for their safety and carries a state prison sentence." This measure went on to become law in all fifty states as of 2019.

THE MURDER OF GARY TRIANO

THE CAR BOMB THAT ROCKED TUCSON

Tucson native Gary Triano made his fortune in Native American bingo businesses and slot machines, both in Arizona and in California, in the time prior to tribes owning and operating their own casinos. Over the years, he became well known in the community as a high-powered developer. Little did he realize when he married his second wife, Pamela Anne Phillips, in 1986 that he had signed his own death sentence.

Gary and Pamela stayed married until 1993. Just a year before their split, the couple purchased a $2 million life insurance policy for Gary, payable to their two children, but with Pamela as their trustee. They were reported to have lived a luxurious lifestyle throughout their marriage, hobnobbing with the elite of Tucson's business community and even meeting Donald Trump before he became president, with then-wife Marla Maples. The well-to-do couple celebrated the birth of their two children soon after their marriage, which made for a large family of children when combined with two children from Triano's first marriage. Phillips became a stay-at-home mom as well, although Triano funded an astrology website she launched called Star Babies, according to NBC News reports. Life wasn't to remain idyllic for the couple, however, and their relationship began to fray at the edges.

Police reports prior to their 1993 divorce indicated a turbulent home life. The local newspaper, in subsequent investigative articles, learned that the two had filed restraining orders against each other on more than one occasion. The divorce didn't end their strife, as it soon led to fights over child support and visitation, the latter after Pamela relocated to Aspen, Colorado, from Tucson. She didn't inform her husband of the move at the time, according to reports. Pamela, oddly enough, did continue monthly payment on her ex-husband's life insurance policy. An exposé on Dateline later revealed that Triano had tried to have the policy canceled but couldn't make any changes to it without Pamela's consent. Her website continued after the move as well. Her Aspen neighbor at the time, Ronald Young, was believed to be an employee.

The divorce and custody matters weren't the only problems on Gary's plate. Within a year of his split, he filed for bankruptcy and was accused of defaulting on loans and not paying a number of large bills as they came due. According to court records and various news accounts of his death, Triano was in debt to the tune of at least $40 million in 1994. Even his dues at the La Paloma Country Club in Tucson, where he golfed, were in trouble. Meanwhile, the fights with his second ex-wife continued.

The country club is located in the Catalina Foothills, on Sunrise Drive in Tucson; the private club today offers members a renovated clubhouse, pool facilities, six dining areas and a twenty-seven-hole golf course. As of November 1, 1996, his membership had not yet been pulled, and Triano enjoyed a game of golf at the sprawling club before heading home. That day, he drove a Lincoln town car that he had borrowed.

A blue canvas bag sat in the passenger seat of the vehicle when Triano climbed into the car that day. It's believed that a pipe bomb was detonated via remote control just as Triano opened the bag to see how it had found its way into his car. The explosion, a combination of the pipe bomb and gunpowder, killed him instantly. Debris scattered over a one-hundred-yard radius, including pieces of the car that were found in the club's swimming pool.

At the time of his death, Triano was nearing his fifty-third birthday. His friends, in fact, had arranged a surprise birthday party for him the day he died. Shortly after his death, Pamela came into a large sum of money thanks to the life insurance policy she had on Gary, but the police had not yet pinned the murder on her. Some believed at the time that the murder may have, in fact, been a mob hit due to the nature of the crime.

That changed as the investigation into the car bombing progressed, particularly when Young rose to the surface as a suspect in the murder. Nearly one month before Triano was killed at the country club, police in

Yorba Linda, California, were investigating a van that would be linked to the Arizona blast that killed the well-known local developer. The abandoned van had been rented by Ronald Young, and inside they found an assortment of items directly tied to Pamela and Gary, including their divorce paperwork and a list of people known to Triano, including what kind of cars they drove. Investigators also found a shotgun and a taser, as well as a receipt for a hotel near Triano's home in Arizona in which he'd spent almost three weeks. Those three weeks, police suspected, were used to tail Pamela's ex-husband and gather information on his movements. The only problem was that while the abandoned van had been found, Young himself had virtually disappeared.

Meanwhile, the car bomb made the news not just in Tucson but across the nation. During this period, police suspected Pamela's involvement but could not officially link her to the crime, despite her connection to Young. Papers had also been found among Young's possessions that indicated that the two could have been romantically involved, although Phillips denied those allegations. By 2005, Young still hadn't been found, leading to a plea on the television show *America's Most Wanted* for information as to his whereabouts. This brought a plausible tip that led to his discovery in Florida, where he was subsequently arrested on a weapons charge. This allowed investigators to seize his possessions, finally allowing them to connect Pamela with Young in a substantive way. Among his possessions were details of a $400,000 payment she made to Young, e-mails and even recordings of the two of them discussing the crime. By 2008, both she and Young had been indicted in connection with Triano's murder.

By this time, however, Pamela had fled to Europe. She managed to elude capture for just over a year but was eventually located in Vienna, Austria, and extradited to the United States for trial.

Young, meanwhile, was sentenced to two life terms without parole after he was found guilty of first-degree murder and conspiracy to commit murder. It would be eighteen years after Triano's death before his ex-wife would face a jury of her peers. The case faced delays when it was found that Pamela was mentally unfit to stand trial, although she was later cleared to appear. She was quickly found guilty of first-degree murder and conspiracy to commit murder just as Young had been. The jury deliberated for less than three days, according to newspaper reports. One month later, she was sentenced to spend the remainder of her natural life behind bars. She's currently living out her sentence in a Phoenix correctional facility.

"I just want everyone to know that I am innocent. I am innocent. I am innocent." According to reports, these are the words Pamela declared to the court after her conviction. She insisted during the trial that the $400,000 she paid to Young was for a business venture and not payment for a hit.

The murder and subsequent trial created a media firestorm and can still be found on a number of true crime shows, including on Oxygen and the ID Channel.

LURED TO THEIR DEATHS

THE INTERNET AND CRIME

While the Internet has been around for decades, with the first iteration of interconnected computers having arrived in the 1960s, it wasn't always available to the public at large. The first working prototype, funded by the U.S. Department of Defense, was known as the advanced Research Projects Agency Network (ARPAnet). While it didn't work well, the first messages were successfully sent to two computers the size of a home; the technology would continue to evolve into the 1970s. This decade would see the creation of the Transmission Control Protocol and Internet Protocol (TCP/IP). When in 1983 ARPAnet adopted the model as well, the modern Internet was born. In the '90s, Tim Berners-Lee created the World Wide Web, which became the most common method for access to websites via the Internet. The Web made the information online accessible to households and individuals across the world.

Cybercrimes, however, had already begun. Before many even had access to the Web, there were those who sought to create mayhem through technology—beginning with the first cybercriminal, hacker Ian Murphy, known as "Captain Zap." In 1981, he hacked into AT&T and changed its internal clock, which might not seem like a big deal—only it charged off-hour rates to phone users during peak demand times and cost the company a ton of money. He ultimately became the first to be convicted for a cybercrime.

Often the Web has been used for even more nefarious, and deadly, purposes. Former medical student Philip Markoff became known as the "Craigslist Killer" for the murder of Julissa Brisman. The 2009 killing, at a hotel in the Boston area of Massachusetts, would highlight the dangers of online interactions. Markoff would later commit suicide in prison in 2010.

Tucson residents were already aware of those dangers, however, when Brian Ferry was arrested for the murder of two Phoenix residents who had traveled south to buy a motorcycle. In 2002, Ferry posted an ad for the motorcycle that drew the attention of Charles Russell and Catherine Nelson. The two made their way to Tucson in their truck on February 2 of that year and were never heard from again. By February 6, they were reported missing after the two failed to report to work, and authorities began a search for the missing couple. They quickly located their vehicle in the parking lot of a Tucson church located on East Twenty-Second Street and South Sixth Avenue.

Their disappearance was officially called a missing persons case, and although foul play was suspected, it went unsolved for years—that is, until new leads emerged that led to Ferry's arrest. At the time of his apprehension, investigators stated that Ferry carried on him a number of "burner" phones, which he used to lure victims to his residence. Authorities also believe that Ferry's father helped him dispose of "household" items a few days after the couple went missing. Ferry's DNA was also found in the victims' truck.

Because the bodies of the missing couple were never found, Ferry's legal counsel claimed that there was a sufficient lack of evidence that the two were indeed killed. The judge presiding over the case declared a mistrial in 2018 when the jury found that it could not reach a verdict, although Ferry was later convicted in May of that year. He was found guilty on two counts of murder on May 16, 2018.

Ferry, according to news reports, was later found unresponsive in his cell at the Pima County Adult Detention Complex. He was pronounced dead after attempts to resuscitate him failed. The death was pronounced a suicide by homicide detectives.

BIZARRE CASE RATTLES TUCSON

EYE SURGEON STABBED TO DEATH OUTSIDE HIS PLACE OF WORK

It was a case of professional jealousy that left Tucson residents rattled in October 2004. This was when the body of local eye surgeon Dr. David Brian Stidham was found outside of his First Avenue business by evening staff. He was still dressed in his work scrubs. Stidham had been stabbed sixteen times and his skull fractured. The deceased, thirty-seven, was a married father of two.

His murder near the Catalina Foothills became big news in the Tucson community and was covered extensively by the media. The story was also featured nationally on the CBS Show *48 Hours* and on Investigation Discovery, and it would be made into an episode for the *Forensic Files* television program. Local reporter A.J. Flick also turned the story into a 2018 true crime book titled *Toxic Rage: A Tale of Murder in Tucson*.

Following the murder, investigators quickly located a suspect in Ronald Bruce Bigger, a homeless man from Indiana, whom they learned had been hired to kill Stidham. The murder-for-hire plot was intended to look like a carjacking, although the true reason centered on professional jealousy.

Pediatric ophthalmologist Bradley Schwartz, investigators learned, hired Bigger to commit the murder. Stidham had gone to work for Schwartz in 2001, but their relationship quickly soured after Schwartz was indicted on drug charges stemming from illegal prescriptions. Schwartz was accused of writing prescriptions for two individuals, his office manager and his then girlfriend, a local attorney, who then gave the pharmaceutical drugs back to Schwartz for his own use. Stidham left the practice after the indictment. He quickly laid the groundwork to begin his own practice across town. When some of Schwartz's patients began to see Stidham, Schwartz became convinced that the doctor was purposely stealing his patients. He went so far as to tell his then girlfriend that he intended to kill him. His romantic partner, Lourdes Lopez, eventually shared this story with Paul Skitzki, a fellow Pima County prosecutor.

An investigation revealed that Schwartz hired Bigger, who was already wanted in Indiana, for $10,000 to carry out the deed. The two are believed to have met either at his medical practice or at a meeting of Narcotics Anonymous. The hired killer had been convicted on a number of charges in the past, including possession of marijuana, check deception and criminal recklessness. By October 15, Bigger was found hiding out near Tucson and promptly arrested. Due to a quick investigation, Schwartz was also arrested that night, according to police reports. Bigger's DNA had been found on the radio knob on the murdered man's vehicle.

The night of the murder, according to numerous accounts, saw Schwartz on a date. As he dined with a new romantic interest at a local Thai restaurant, Biggers showed up to see Schwartz, and the two spoke cryptically to each other in front of the woman, according to reports. He introduced the man as "Bruce" to his date, although she suspected that he might have been involved in Stidman's death. She confronted Schwartz regarding her concerns the following day. He denied involvement in the murder, but she reported the incident to the police anyway. Police eventually connected Biggers and Schwartz via phone records and discovered that the two had been in contact multiple times. One call placed to the doctor's cellphone came from a restaurant pay phone across the street from the murder scene. The two were charged with first-degree murder and conspiracy to commit first-degree murder. Both men claimed that they were not guilty. Schwartz was eventually convicted in 2006 and sentenced to twenty-five years to life for the conspiracy charge. Biggers, meanwhile, was sentenced to life in prison in 2007 without the possibility of parole.

Since his incarceration, Schwartz would remain in the news cycle due to a series of incidents in which he was assaulted by other inmates. Schwartz sued the State of Arizona over the attacks. His one-time girlfriend, meanwhile, resigned for her role in the murder-for-hire plot. Lopez was also later disbarred for her part in the prescription fraud scheme. Stidham's widow, meanwhile, sued the medical complex where her husband was murdered for not providing sufficient conditions to prevent the killing. She also sued Pima County, believing that it could have done more to prevent the murder with its prior knowledge of Schwartz's intention, particularly involving Lopez and Skitzki.

HOME INVASION TERROR

THE ARIVACA INCIDENT

On May 30, 2011, the Flores-Gonzalez family faced a trio of home invaders when a group barged into their home after the family had all turned in for the night. They were woken around 1:00 a.m., according to news reports of the incident. They believed that police were at their door. Brisenia Flores, nine, slept on the couch that night to be near the family's new dog, and her father, Raul, and mother, Gina Gonzalez, rushed into the room to intercept what they believed to be officers of the law. Their other daughter was spending the night at a friend's home.

The so-called vigilante incident occurred in the unincorporated community of Arivaca, located just south of Tucson near the Mexico border. In 2000, the community had a population of fewer than one thousand individuals. Besides being eleven miles from the border, it's also known for being the home of more than one hundred mines.

Jason Eugene Bush, Shawna Forde and Albert Robert Gaxiola were members of a Washington-based militia organization that conducted border patrols in Arizona as part of their anti–illegal immigration efforts. The three dressed as law enforcement officers to commit what many say was originally meant to be armed robbery, although other accounts differ on the incident. According to news accounts, the group planned to fund their militia operation by holding up people they suspected of trafficking in illegal drugs or harboring undocumented immigrants. They expected to find a lot of cash in the home, authorities said at the time, due to Raul's alleged drug connections, which they planned to use on their fledgling anti-immigration operations. Some claim that the trio went in planning more than just a robbery and intended from the beginning to murder everyone in the home to ensure that there would be no witnesses.

Upon entering the trailer home, it was reported, Bush killed Raul and his daughter and wounded Gina, who played dead to avoid further injury. Gina later told jurors that Raul questioned the identity of the invaders, and that is when the shooting began. The fake officers told the family that they were searching for fugitives in the area. The three left the residence after murdering her family, and Gina called authorities only to find, to her horror, that the group returned. Armed with a pistol, she fired at the trio while on the phone with 911 dispatchers, striking Bush in the leg. He was later arrested in Kingman, Arizona, when he sought medical treatment. All three were charged with two counts of first-degree murder. While hoping to find cash, the group allegedly left with only jewelry. That jewelry was later recovered in Forde's vehicle, according to law enforcement. Forde became one of only two other women on Arizona's death row in 2011.

Forde was said to be the ringleader of the group and planned the attacks, witnesses said. She denied involvement in planning the murders. Gaxiola and Bush also denied involvement in the murders. Forde was once a member of the Minuteman Civil Defense Corps, although she was considered something of a black sheep among other members of the organization. She eventually left the group to found her own border protection organization, the Minutemen American Defense, where she recruited like-minded individuals to her plans. According to some accounts, there were fourteen members of the organization at the time of the murders.

During the subsequent trial, it was revealed that Forde had gone so far as to draw a map of the attack, which she shared with potential recruits on a trip to Colorado. Those potential recruits shared the map with the FBI, although the information was allegedly not acted on in a timely matter when it was passed to the Bureau's Phoenix office; any preemptive actions it might have triggered did not prevent the murders. Gonzalez later sued the FBI over the issue, although the case was eventually tossed out of court.

THE GABBY GIFFORDS SHOOTING

SIX KILLED IN GROCERY STORE PARKING LOT

Just after 10:00 a.m. on the morning of January 8, 2011, Arizona State Representative Gabrielle Giffords set out to meet with her constituents in the parking lot of a Safeway grocery store in Casas Adobe, a community within the Tucson metropolitan area. The sunny Arizona morning began like many others for Giffords and her staff as they set up a table outside the grocery store and began to meet with concerned citizens. It wasn't long after that 911 dispatchers began to receive calls of gunshots at the scene.

Giffords hosted the "Congress on Your Corner" event to chat with residents in her southern Arizona district, just as many politicians do across the country. A small gathering of under thirty individuals made their way to meet her, and she arrived a few minutes before 10:00 a.m. Twenty-two-year-old Jared Loughner also arrived around that time, after taking a taxi to the grocery store from his parents' house where he lived. Surveillance cameras captured him as he entered the store and approached the table to see Giffords. He drew a Glock 19 semi-automatic pistol and began shooting.

Giffords was shot in the head at point-blank range. Loughner then turned the gun on others at the table, killing six and injuring thirteen. Among those killed were nine-year-old Christina-Taylor Green, Giffords staffer Gabe Zimmerman, Phyllis Schneck, Dorothy Morris, Dorwan Stoddard and U.S. District Judge John Roll. Loughner was tackled to the ground when he stopped shooting to reload, according to news accounts. One of his subduers, retired U.S. Army colonel Bill Badger, seventy-four, was also one of Loughner's

Convicted killer Jared Loughner during his booking by U.S. marshals in Phoenix, Arizona. Loughner killed six people during a 2011 public meet-and-greet event in Tucson. *U.S. Marshals Service.*

Former representative Gabby Giffords was awarded the Army Decoration for Distinguished Civilian Service in 2013 after stepping down from her Congressional role. *U.S. Army.*

victims. Others quickly rushed to Badger's aid, including Patricia Maisch, who snatched up Loughner's loaded magazine when he dropped it to the ground. The gunman carried four magazines with him that fateful day, two of which were reportedly able to carry thirty-three rounds of ammunition. Thirty-one shell casings were recovered at the scene. The first emergency call was made about one minute after the incident occurred.

Daniel Hernandez Jr. is credited with saving Giffords's life that fateful day by tending to her injuries until paramedics arrived. A married doctor and nurse, who happened to be shopping in the grocery store, immediately sprang into action as well, working to tend to Loughner's victims until help arrived. Media initially reported that Giffords had died as a result of the shooting, although they soon corrected that statement when it was revealed she still lived, though in critical condition. Many of the wounded were taken to Tucson's University Medical Center. Five people died at the scene, with Green passing away while en route to the hospital.

Police immediately locked down the area and cordoned off Loughner's home. It was discovered that Loughner had met Giffords a handful of years before the shooting while he was a student at the northwest campus of Pima Community College. Among items seized from his parents' home were notes found in a safe that were marked with the words "I planned ahead," "My assassination" and "Giffords." He was eventually convicted on several counts, including murder, and sentenced to seven life terms in prison. Giffords's husband, astronaut Mark Kelly, directed a comment at Loughner during the court proceedings: "You have decades upon decades to contemplate what you did, but after today, at this moment, here and now, Gabby and I are done thinking about you." Loughner was sentenced on November 8, 2012. Kelly went on to run for the U.S. Senate in 2020.

Giffords herself faced a long road to recovery. She stepped down from her role in Congress a year after the incident and now spends her efforts combating gun violence in the country alongside her husband. During the emergency surgery directly following the incidents, doctors had to remove part of her skull to prevent brain damage caused by swelling. Surprisingly, following a medically induced coma, she was deemed able to be released from the hospital two short weeks after the attack and entered rehabilitation therapy. She suffers from issues with her eyesight and with language as a result of her injuries.

Loughner, who refused to talk to authorities, never expressed a clear motive for the attack. Speculation about his reasoning ran wild in the media and in political circles, from mental illness to pure political spite. He was later diagnosed with paranoid schizophrenia.

BIBLIOGRAPHY

ABC 15 Arizona. "Prisoner Killed Girlfriend, Had Sex with Corpse." www.abc15.com.

ABC News. "Border Vigilante Shawna Forde Sentenced to Death for Home Invasion." https://abcnews.go.com.

ADOT. "Monsoons." www.azdot.gov.

American Battlefields Trust. "Picacho Peak Picacho Pass." www.battlefields.org.

Arizona Daily Star. "Butterfly Trail: Beauty and the Butterfly." www.tucson.com.

———. "Cold Cases: Unsolved Murders in Southern Arizona." www.tucson.com.

———. "Drama in Time: Louise Foucar Marshall Left Her Mark on Tucson." www.tucson.com.

———. "Louis Taylor, of Notorious Pioneer Hotel Fire Case, Accused of Armed Robbery." www.tucson.com.

———. "Metal-Detecting Discovery in Tucson Leads to Bridge's Name." www.tucson.com.

———. "1967: Jet Crashes into Food Giant." www.tucson.com.

———. "Photos: Bombings in Tucson in 1968." www.tucson.com.

———. "Photos: Tucson's First 'Gangland-Style' Murder in 1960." www.tucson.com.

———. "Tales from the Morgue: Fire in the Opera House." www.tucson.com.

———. "Tales from the Morgue: 47 Years Ago the Pioneer Hotel Burned in Tucson." www.tucson.com.

———. "Taylor Embraces Freedom 42 Years after Pioneer Fire." www.tucson.com.

———. "Unhappy Editor Admits He 'Killed' Old Santa." www.tucson.com.

Arizona Department of Corrections Rehabilitation & Reentry. "Arizona Death Penalty History." www.corrections.az.gov.

Black Past. "Tucson Race Riot (1967)." www.blackpast.org.

Britannica. "University of Arizona." www.britannica.com.

Bruns, Richard. *I, a Squealer: The Insider's Account of the Pied Piper of Tucson Murders*. Tucson, AZ: Twin Feathers Publishing, 2018.

CBS News. "One-Time Socialite Guilty in Car Bomb Killing of Ex-Husband." www.cbsnews.com.

City of Tucson. "Floods and Flash Floods." www.tucsonaz.gov.

Davis-Monthan Air Force Base. "About DM." www.dm.af.mil.

Eppinga, Jane. *Tucson, Arizona*. Charleston, SC: Arcadia Publishing, 2000.

Federal Bureau of Investigation (FBI). "John Dillinger." www.fbi.gov.

Gangster Report. "Going Bananas in the Bonannos: The Banana Mob War Timeline (1964–1969)." www.gangsterreport.com.

Good Housekeeping. "How Rebecca Schaeffer's Horrific Murder Led to the Nation's First Anti-Stalking Law." www.goodhousekeeping.com.

History.com. "Civil Rights Act of 1964." www.history.com.

———. "Geronimo." www.history.com.

———. "Pearl Harbor." www.history.com.

———. "Spanish Flu." www.history.com.

HuffPost. "Here's Why You Shouldn't Jump to Conclusions about Mass Shooters' Motivations." www.huffpost.com.

KOLD News 13. "Convicted Murderer Brian Ferry Found Dead in Jail Cell." www.kold.com.

Los Angeles Times. "Fan Convicted of Murder in Actress Slaying: Trial: Judge Also Rules that the Obsessed Robert Bardo Lay in Wait for Rebecca Schaeffer, Requiring a Sentence of Life in Prison without the Possibility of Parole." www.latimes.com.

———. "Inmate Stabs Killer of Actress." www.latimes.com.

The Marshall Foundation. "About Louise." www.marshallfoundation.com.

Military.com. "First Battle of Tucson." www.military.wikia.org.

Murderpedia. "Eva Dugan." www. murderpedia.org.

National Park Service. "San Xavier del Bac Mission Arizona." www.nps.gov.

National Weather Service. "Tropical Storm Octave 1983." www.wrh.noaa.gov.

New York Times. "The Arizona Shooting, and What Led Up to It." www.archive.nytimes.com.

Northern Arizona University. "Arizona Heritage Waters." www.azheritagewaters.nau.edu.

Norton, Clark. *Secret Tucson: A Guide to the Weird, Wonderful, and Obscure*. St. Louis, MO: Reedy Press, LLC, 2019.

O.K. Corral. "A Brief History of the Famous Gunfight at the O.K. Corral." www.ok-corral.com.

Officer Down Memorial Page. "Tucson Police Department." www.odmp.org.

Pima County Public Library. "Flash Flood Deaths in the Tucson Area." www.library.pima.gov.

———. "Man Who Killed Santa Claus, John McPhee." www.library.pima.gov.

The Times. "America's Own Robin Hood: The Dillinger Legend." www.thetimes.co.uk.

True West Magazine. "Eva Dugan: The Only Woman Hanged in Arizona." www.truewestmagazine.com.

Tucson Historic Preservation Foundation. "1918 Spanish Flu: Heroes on UA Campus." www.preservetucson.org.

Tucson Weekly. "The Murder of Dr. David Stidham." www.tucsonweekly.com.

U.S. News. "50 Years After Race Riots, Issues Remain the Same." www.usnews.com.

———. "Race Troubles: 109 U.S. Cities Faced Violence in 1967." www.usnews.com.

USA Today. "FBI Releases New Photos, Video of 2011 Gabby Giffords Shooting." https://www.usatoday.com.

USS *Arizona* Facts. "In Honor of James Randolf Van Horn." www.ussarizonafacts.org.

Worldcat. "Fieldnotes from the Arizona Bureau of Geology and Mineral Technology." https://www.worldcat.org.

ABOUT THE AUTHOR

Patrick Whitehurst is a fiction and nonfiction writer. He's the author of the Barker Mysteries novellas and three books in the Images of America series. His most recent book, *Haunted Monterey County*, reveals the many ghostly locations found in the Central Coast community. His short stories have appeared in *Shotgun Honey*, *Switchblade Magazine* and *Hoosier Noir*. His book reviews and author interviews can be found at *Suspense Magazine*. As a journalist, he's covered everything from the deaths of nineteen Granite Mountain Hotshots to President Barack Obama's visit to the Grand Canyon. Patrick lives in Tucson, Arizona. Visit him online at patrickwhitehurst.com.